LONGMAN PRACTICE NOTES

# BUSINESS TENANCIES

1ST EDITION

Chris Hugill
*Solicitor*

SERIES EDITOR

CM Brand, Solicitor and Lecturer in Law
University of Liverpool

ISBN 0851 21531 9

*Published by*
Longman Law, Tax and Finance
Longman Group UK Ltd
21/27 Lamb's Conduit Street
London WC1N 3NJ

*Associated offices*:
Australia, Hong Kong, Malaysia, Singapore, USA



A CIP catalogue record for this book is available from the British Library

Typeset by
The Word Shop, Rossendale, Lancs

Printed and bound in Great Britain by
Biddles Ltd, Guildford and King's Lynn

# CONTENTS


1 **Basic Information**

| | | |
|---|---|---|
| 1.1 | Introduction | 1 |
| 1.2 | Sources | 1 |
| 1.3 | When to have a contract | 2 |
| 1.4 | The need for a deed | 3 |
| 1.5 | When to deduce title | 4 |
| 1.6 | Who pays the costs | 4 |
| 1.7 | Value Added TAX and business leases | 5 |
| 1.8 | Glossary | 6 |
| 1.9 | Court jurisdiction | 9 |

2 **Time Limits and Court Fees**

| | | |
|---|---|---|
| 2.1 | Grant and assignment | 10 |
| 2.2 | Landlord and Tenant Act 1954, Part II | 11 |
| 2.3 | Compensation for improvements | 12 |
| 2.4 | Leasehold Property Repairs Act 1938 | 12 |
| 2.5 | Rent review | 13 |
| 2.6 | Options | 13 |
| 2.7 | Court fees | 13 |

3 **Statutory Renewal and Rent Review**

| | | |
|---|---|---|
| 3.1 | Landlord and Tenant Act 1954, Part II | 14 |
| 3.2 | Rent Review | 20 |

4 **Drafting the Lease**

| | | |
|---|---|---|
| 4.1 | The preamble | 25 |
| 4.2 | The description | 25 |
| 4.3 | Tenant's rights and landlord's exceptions and reservations | 26 |
| 4.4 | Length of term | 27 |
| 4.5 | Rent | 27 |
| 4.6 | Tenant's covenants | 27 |
| 4.7 | Landlord's covenants | 29 |
| 4.8 | The Service charge | 30 |
| 4.9 | Provisos | 32 |

5 **Procedural Checklists**

5.1 Grant of lease 34
5.2 Assignment of lease 40
5.3 Surrender 44

6 **Landlord's Consent**

6.1 General 46
6.2 Assignment and sub-letting 47
6.3 Alterations 50
6.4 User 52

7 **Precedents**

7.1 Rent review clause 53
7.2 Rent review trigger notice 57
7.3 Tenancy at will 58
7.4 Forms in connection with a joint application to the county court for an order under s 38(4) of the Landlord and Tenant Act 1954, Part II 60
7.5 Statutory renewal forms 64
7.6 Declaration that the Landlord has unreasonably witheld consent to assignment of lease and change of user 86
7.7 Licence permitting assignment 89
7.8 Deed of surrender of a registered lease 92

8 **Common Practical Problems** 95

9 **Further Reading** 97
9.1 Looseleaf works 97
9.2 Books 97

*The forms appearing in section 7.5 of this book are based upon Oyez forms and are reproduced by kind permission of The Solicitors' Law Stationery Society Ltd.*

# PREFACE

This book contains an outline of the law and practice relating to business leases. I have tried to refer to other sources where appropriate and would emphasise that all practitioners operating in this field should consult the primary sources of the Green Book, White Book and the various statutory provisions wherever they may be relevant. Volume 22 of the Encyclopaedia of Forms and Precedents also constitutes an essential tool in this field.

Practitioners are required to understand the workings of Value Added Tax (to a greater extent than previously) and in this connection the Finance Act 1989 is an essential read. In such complex areas I have merely been able to point readers in the right direction.

I have endeavoured to state the law as at 31 May 1989. At that time the Finance Act 1989 was merely a Bill and readers should check the Act to ensure that the position with regard to VAT remains unchanged.

Also s 2 of the Law of Property (Miscellaneous Provisions) Act 1989, came into force on 27 September 1989 after this book was written. This provides that a contract for the sale or other disposition of an interest in land can only be made in writing and only by incorporating all the terms which have been expressly agreed in one document or in each document where contracts are exchanged. The terms may be incorporated in a document by being set out in it or by reference to some other document and the document, or one of the documents incorporating the terms where contracts are exchanged (but not necessarily the same one), must be signed by or on behalf of each party. The section does not apply, amongst other things, to leases of three years or less falling within LPA 1926, s 54(2). Section 40 of the Law of Property Act 1925 is abolished and all references to the effects of that provision in this book, including paras 1.3, 5.1 and 5.2, should be read in the light of these changes. It is suggested that the precautions mentioned in sub-para 1.3 may still be taken to prevent creating an agreed express term whose absence from the formal contract may invalidate the whole contract. Care should be taken to make reference in the contract to any 'side letter' containing contract terms.

Chris Hugill
1989

CHAPTER 1

# BASIC INFORMATION

## 1.1 Introduction

This book provides a guide to various practical aspects of business leases, in particular grant, renewal and assignment. Such matters constitute an important part of the work of the commercial conveyancer, but also feature frequently in the daily life of a general practice lawyer. Although this book refers more often to solicitors, it is appreciated that licensed conveyancers may also be involved in this kind of commercial work. The term 'solicitor' should therefore, strictly for the purpose of this book, be regarded as also applying to a licensed conveyancer.

Due to constraints of space, knowledge of basic conveyancing procedures as set out in RM Coates, *Conveyancing*, 1st edn (Longman, 1988) must be assumed. Other titles in this series which may assist the reader are CM Brand, *Planning Law*, 1st edn (Longman, 1989) and R Colbey, *Residential Tenancies*, 1st edn (Longman, 1988).

## 1.2 Sources

**1.2.1 Statutes** The most important enactment is the Landlord and Tenant Act 1954, Pt II, granting most business tenants security of tenure and giving rise to issues which must be considered before, during and near the end of a commercial lease. Apart from the ubiquitous Law of Property Act (LPA) 1925, and other 1925 property legislation, other important statutes include the Landlord and Tenant Acts 1927 and 1988 and the Law of Property Act 1969. However, the law relating to business leases is not as dependent on statutory sources as residential leases.

**1.2.2 Delegated legislation** As with residential landlord and tenant law, delegated legislation deals mainly with forms and procedure and the most important are:

- County Court Rules 1981 (SI 1981 No 1687).
- Landlord and Tenant Act 1954 (Appropriate Multiplier) Order 1984 (SI 1984 No 1932).
- Landlord and Tenant (Determination of Rateable Value Procedure) Rules 1954 (SI 1954 No 1255).

- Landlord and Tenant Act 1954, Pt II (Notices) (Amendment) Regulations 1989 (SI 1989 No 1548).
- Rules of the Supreme Court (Revision) 1965 (SI 1965 No 1776).

**1.2.3 Case law** The decisions of the courts provide an important source in this area and, in addition to the major law reports, specialist reports such as those found weekly in the Estates Gazette are essential reading. This is particularly important with regard to matters such as rent reviews and dilapidations.

## 1.3 When to have a contract

**1.3.1 Inadvertent contracts** If correspondence contains details of the parties, price, property and any other agreed terms, then there is a possibility that this will either constitute a contract or a memorandum of an oral contract. In both cases there will be an enforceable contract (LPA 1925, s 40). On the grant or assignment of a lease, both parties' solicitors should ensure that their correspondence and that of their clients and other agents contains the words 'Subject to Contract' (if one is envisaged), or 'Subject to Lease', or even 'Subject to Contract and Lease'. As there is always a danger that these words will be omitted from correspondence, the better practice is to add a paragraph to the first letter to the other side along the following lines:

> We would point out that, prior to the grant of the lease by formal exchange of the lease and counterpart, first, our client has no intention of entering into a binding and enforceable contract or lease and, secondly, neither this firm, our client nor anyone else has authority to commit it to such a contract or lease. Until this grant by formal exchange has taken place, all correspondence (inclusive of this letter) from this firm, our client or anyone else on its behalf is subject to contract and lease.

The other side's solicitor will usually be pleased to respond as follows:

> The final paragraph of your letter dated . . . should also be regarded as incorporated in this letter.

The paragraph itself will need to be adapted if there is to be an exchange of contracts prior to the lease, or where the transaction is an assignment of the residue of an existing lease.

**1.3.2 Grant of a lease** It is unusual for the parties to enter into a formal contract prior to a lease, save where there are special reasons. Thus, no lease may be possible until some event has occurred, such as obtaining planning permission for proposed alterations, or the head landlord's consent to the underletting. Alternatively, the premises may not yet have been built and an agreement is necessary to regulate the manner of their construction.

In such circumstances, the precise form of the lease should be resolved and attached to the agreement prior to exchange of contracts rather than to create potential uncertainty by providing that the lease will be for a certain term of years and rent and otherwise subject to the 'usual covenants'. It is now apparent that these usual covenants can vary in each particular case (see *Chester* v *Buckingham Travel Ltd* [1981] 1 WLR 96).

**1.3.3 Assignment** It is standard practice to enter into a formal contract prior to legal completion of the assignment. The contract may be conditional upon the landlord's licence to assign being granted. See Coates (op cit p 35) with regard to the drafting of the contract.

**1.3.4 Surrender** Where there is to be a straightforward surrender of a lease, there is little point in having an agreement prior to the deed though, if there is one (as with a grant and assignment), it must comply with LPA 1925, s 40 to be enforceable. Sometimes a lease will require that the tenant shall offer to surrender the lease in certain circumstances (eg before seeking consent to an assignment). However, an agreement to surrender a lease protected by the 1954 Act would be void under s 38(1) (*Bocardo SA* v *S and M Hotels Ltd* [1980] 1 WLR 17). The court may, on the joint application of the landlord and tenant (but not, it seems, before commencement of the lease), authorise an agreement to surrender a business lease (s 38(4)).

## 1.4 The need for a deed

**1.4.1 Grant** A deed must be used to create a legal lease for a term exceeding three years (LPA 1925, s 52(1)). However, a lease for not more than three years taking effect in possession at the best rent reasonably obtainable without taking a fine, may be merely in writing or even oral (s 54(2)). Because of their duration, business leases are invariably created by deed.

**1.4.2 Assignment** To pass a legal estate, an assignment of a lease must always be by deed (LPA 1925, s 52(1)).

**1.4.3 Surrender** An express surrender of a legal lease should always be by deed (LPA 1925, s 52(1)). However, informal surrenders by operation of law are also effective and, indeed, common in practice (eg where the old lease has been superseded by a new one granted to the same tenant).

## 1.5 When to deduce title

**1.5.1 Grant of a lease** The landlord is not obliged to deduce title to the freehold (LPA 1925, s 44(2)) and s 110 of the Land Registration Act 1925 does not apply where the superior title is registered. On the grant of a sub-lease out of an unregistered lease, the lease out of which it is to be derived and, where appropriate, all dispositions under which the lease has been held during the last fifteen years must be proved. As a contract is unusual, these rules are not that significant in practice. The tenant should insist in all cases on superior titles being proved, though the landlord may wish to resist this, particularly if the term is relatively short. Where there is a contract, the tenant's solicitor should add appropriate special conditions to improve the tenant's position.

The risks involved in not obtaining proof of superior titles are:

- The landlord may not have a good title and have no legal right to grant a lease.
- There may be a mortgage precluding leasing and the mortgagee's consent will be needed.
- There may be third party rights such as restrictive covenants and easements adversely affecting the premises.

**1.5.2 Assignment** If the title is unregistered, the assignor must prove the lease and all dispositions under which it has been held during the last fifteen years. If title is registered, the assignor proves its immediate title in the usual way by office copy entries of the register of title and filed plan, an authority to inspect the register and a copy of the lease (see LRA 1925, s 110). The Law Society's Conditions of Sale (LSC) improve the assignee's position by providing that the assignor must prove all superior titles where the lease was dated not more than fifteen years before the contract for a term exceeding twenty-one years (LSC 8(2)). The assignee's solicitor should always consider the need for a special condition to gain additional rights to investigate superior titles.

**1.5.3 Surrender** There is rarely a contract and no rules as to what title each party must prove. However, the landlord will usually require that the tenant proves its title and, in particular, the landlord will want to satisfy itself that there is no mortgage affecting the property. The tenant should also ask for proof of the landlord's title.

## 1.6 Who pays the costs

**1.6.1 Grant of a lease** The landlord will normally be able to use its superior bargaining position to obtain the tenant's agreement that the landlord's legal charges will be met by the tenant. This will usually be a term of the lease itself and, indeed, the agreement is not enforceable unless it is in writing (Costs of Leases Act 1958, s 1). However, on a renewal under the 1954 Act, the court will not order that such a term be incorporated in the new lease as this would deprive the tenant of the protection of the 1958 Act (*Cairnplace Ltd* v *CBL (Property Investment) Ltd* [1984] 1 WLR 696). When the terms of the lease are negotiated on renewal, the tenant's solicitor should argue, on this basis, that the tenant should not be liable for the landlord's costs. In fact, there is nothing to stop the parties agreeing that such a term be included in the renewed lease.

**1.6.2 Assignment** It is unusual for the assignee to agree to pay the assignor's costs, though this does sometimes occur.

**1.6.3 Surrender** This is a matter for negotiation and much depends on which party most wants the surrender to take place.

**1.6.4 Licences to assign, alter or change user** Where there are qualified covenants allowing the tenant to assign or underlet, to carry out alterations or to change the user with the landlord's consent, the landlord has the right to require payment of its legal or other expenses (1927 Act, s 19) and this will be the landlord's usual practice.

## 1.7 Value Added Tax and business leases

The general principle is that VAT is charged on any supply of goods and services where it is a taxable supply made by a taxable person in the course of a business carried on by that person. The standard rate of VAT is currently 15 per cent. The tax is borne in theory by the final consumer. Registered businesses which are not exempt are entitled to credit for VAT charged to them (known as input tax) on their business purchases of goods and services.

Until the passing of the Finance Act 1989, VAT had not been charged on rents or on premiums payable on the grant or assignment of a lease. From 1 August 1989, landlords who let non-domestic buildings can elect to charge VAT on rents and premiums at the standard rate and can therefore recover input tax on costs attributable to the supply (for a discussion of the effect on rental values see *3.2.3*). The election applies to the whole building, including buildings linked together by a walkway and all of the units in a shopping centre. It is irrevocable and will apply to all supplies by the landlord relating to that building. Thus the election will also apply to the consideration on the eventual sale of the reversion. Similarly, the tenant can elect to charge VAT on the premium payable on the assignment of a lease of a non-domestic building.

There are transitional provisions whereby tenants whose landlords elect to tax leases pay VAT on only half their rent in the first year up to 31 July 1990. The reduction applies to rent relating to that year (or part of that year) provided that the building was completed prior to 1 August 1989. However, where the lease is of land (without buildings) the reduction only applies if the tenant was in occupation immediately before 1 August 1989. For tenants in the above situations who are charities, VAT is charged on 20 per cent of the rent in year one, 40 per cent in year two and so on until VAT is charged on the full rent in year five.

Most tenants will be able to recover this VAT. The main problems are caused for exempt and partly exempt businesses such as charities, banks, insurance companies, private schools and hospitals whose ability to recover the VAT will be restricted. Such tenants may attempt to persuade the landlord to covenant not to make an election to charge VAT on the rents, perhaps in return, covenanting in the lease to reimburse the landlord for irrecoverable input tax arising where the option to charge VAT is not exercised (see *4.6.1*).

It should be noted that there is no option to tax any supply of a house, flat or other qualifying building, or any part of a building which is used in a similar way (save an office used by a charity for non-business purposes).

Distinct from the option to charge VAT is the new rule that from 1 April 1989, the surrender for a consideration of an interest in land (except that domestic accommodation is unlikely to be subject to VAT) is standard rated for VAT. If no reference is made to VAT, then the consideration will be deemed to be inclusive of VAT and the recipient (whether the landlord or the tenant) will suffer a loss by having to account for this out of the inclusive sum received. All deeds of surrender should therefore make it clear that VAT is payable on the consideration (see Precedent *7.6*).

## 1.8 Glossary

**Absolute covenant** A term used commonly in the context of covenants precluding assignment or sub-letting, alterations or a change of user where there is no express provision for the tenant to seek the landlord's consent.

**Arbitrator** A person undertaking a judicial function in resolving a dispute (commonly in a lease to fix the rent pursuant to a rent review clause on the failure of the parties to agree).

**Assignment** Where the tenant transfers the whole of its interest to a third party.

**Assumptions** A word commonly used to describe the terms expressly assumed in a rent review clause, helping to create a hypothetical lease subject to which a rent has to be fixed.

**Best rent** The highest rent that can reasonably be obtained during the term of the lease.

**Break clause** An option in a fixed term lease enabling one or both parties to terminate the lease early by serving a notice to quit.

**Clear lease** A lease in which the tenant bears the costs of repair maintenance and general running costs of the demised premises and therefore all of the uncertain expenditure, and the landlord receives a rent clear of such overheads.

**Competent landlord** The landlord with whom the tenant must conduct the procedure for renewal under the 1954 Act and who is not always the tenant's immediate landlord (see *3.1.3*).

**Demised premises** The property forming the subject matter of the lease.

**Disregards** A term commonly used to describe the matters which a valuer must ignore in calculating the appropriate rent pursuant to a rent review clause or on a statutory renewal.

**Expert** A valuer making a determination relying on his own skill and judgment (commonly as to the appropriate rent pursuant to a rent review clause).

**Fine** A premium or lump sum payment.

**Fitting out period** A time during which a tenant carries out alterations to the demised premises and, in respect of such period, a landlord may agree that the tenant can pay a reduced rent or no rent at all.

**Fixed term tenancy** A tenancy which will end (subject to the 1954 Act) automatically on expiry of the agreed period.

**Forfeiture** A landlord's right to re-enter the demised premises if the tenant is in breach of a covenant in the lease arising where such right is expressly reserved, or the lease is conditional upon observance of the covenants.

**Head lease** A lease where the landlord has a freehold estate as opposed to a lease.

**Holding** For the purposes of the 1954 Act this means the demised premises excluding any part occupied neither by the tenant nor a person employed by the tenant for a business (see *3.1.7*).

**Hypothetical lease** The imaginary lease created by the assumptions and disregards in a rent review clause upon which basis the valuer must calculate the rent.

**Licence** A personal permission to occupy land usually arising where the occupant does not have exclusive possession of the premises or in other exceptional situations. The main consequence of a licence is that the occupant has no security of tenure under the 1954 Act.

**Notice to quit** A notice given by either the landlord or the tenant to terminate a periodic tenancy or a fixed term tenancy containing a break clause.

**Option** A right to have some benefit (to terminate or break the lease, to renew the lease or to purchase the reversion), by serving a notice on the other party.

**Periodic tenancy** A tenancy made for a period of a week, quarter, month or year and determinable by notice to quit.

**Proviso** A condition attached to some term of the lease.

**Quarter days** An annual rent is often expressed to be paid quarterly on the 'usual quarter days' meaning 25 March, 24 June, 29 September, and 25 December.

**Qualified covenant** A term commonly used to describe a covenant precluding assignment or sub-letting, alterations or a change of user without first obtaining the landlord's consent.

**Rent deposit** A sum of money paid by a tenant or assignee as security for the landlord or assignor respectively for non-payment of rent or other breaches of tenancy obligations.

**Rent review** The process of re-assessing the rent at regular intervals during the term of a lease pursuant to the relevant provisions contained in that lease.

**Reversion** The landlord's interest, whether it be a freehold or leasehold estate.

**Root of title** In a leasehold context this is an assignment dealing with the ownership of the whole legal estate and equitable interests, containing an identifiable description and not casting any doubt on the title. The assignment should be at least fifteen years old (LPA 1969, s 24).

**Service charge** The cost apportioned between tenants of the landlord for providing certain services.

**Sinking fund** A fund built up by contributions from tenants, and intended to be utilised for non-recurrent expenses and major items of expenditure incurred by the landlord and recoverable as part of the service charge.

**Statutory renewal** The grant of a new lease to a tenant under the provisions of the 1954 Act.

**Sub-letting** A lease granted out of a longer lease.

**Surrender** The termination of a lease by agreement between the parties.

**Tenancy at will** A tenancy which can be terminated at any time by either party.

**Travelling draft** A draft document such as a lease, sent backwards and forwards between the parties' solicitors to be amended and re-amended.

**Trigger notice** A notice served on the tenant by which the landlord initiates the rent review procedure.

**Usual covenants** These are the covenants which the court will order should be included in a lease where specific performance of a contract for a lease is granted not specifying the precise terms.

**Waste** Spoil or destruction of the premises for which the tenant wll be liable in tort to compensate the landlord.

## 1.9 Court jurisdiction

In many cases the landlord or tenant will wish to bring their action in the county court, rather than the High Court, to keep costs to a minimum. However, various limits tied to rent or rateable value must be observed, and the county court will only have jurisdiction in the following cases:

- Monetary claims up to £5,000 (County Courts Act 1984, s 5).
- Applications under the 1954 Act, Pt II where the rateable value does not exceed £5,000 (1954 Act, s 63(2)). (Note however that a 1954 Act matter can, by agreement in writing between the parties, be transferred from the county court to the High Court, or from the High Court to a county court specified in the agreement, s 63(3).)
- Applications to court for a declaration that a licence to assign or sub-let, to make improvements or to change the user has been unreasonably withheld whatever the net annual value, though the High Court may also have jurisdiction (1954 Act, s 53(1)).
- Application to court by the tenant for authority to carry out improvements under the 1927 Act where the rateable value does not exceed £5,000 (1927 Act, s 21 which provides that s 63 of the 1954 Act shall apply–see above).

CHAPTER 2

# TIME LIMITS AND COURT FEES

## 2.1 Grant and assignment

It is rare to have a contract preceding the grant of a business lease, though invariably on an assignment contracts will be exchanged in the usual way. The contract will normally incorporate either the National Conditions of Sale (20th ed) or the Law Society's Conditions of Sale (1984 Revision) both of which impose a regime of time limits. The table below summarises some of the more important conditions. Although the terms 'assignor' and 'assignee' are used, the words 'landlord' and 'tenant' should be substituted on the grant of a lease, where appropriate.

| | *National conditions* | *Law Society's conditions* |
|---|---|---|
| Assignee pays deposit | On the date of the contract (NC 2(1)) | On or before the date of the contract (LSC 9(1)) |
| Assignor delivers abstract or office copy entries, etc | Not later than 11 working days after the date of the contract (NC 9(1)) | Forthwith upon exchange of contracts (LSC 12(1)) |
| Assignor applies for licence to assign | No time limit and is unclear by what time consent should be obtained (NC 11(5)) | Forthwith and consent should be granted at least 5 working days before contractual completion date. Otherwise assignor or assignee can rescind (LSC 8(4)) |
| Assignee delivers requisitions | Within 11 working days of delivery of abstract (NC 9(3)) | Within 6 working days of delivery of later of abstract or contract (LSC 15(2)) |
| Assignor replies to requisitions | No time limit | Within 4 working days of delivery of requisitions (LSC 15(2)) |

| | | |
|---|---|---|
| Assignee delivers observations on replies | Within 6 working days of replies (NC 9(3)) | Within 4 working days of replies (LSC 15(3)) |
| Assignee delivers draft assignment (no equivalent on grant of lease) | At least 6 working days before completion date (NC 19(3)) | At least 12 working days before contractual completion date (LSC 17(1)) |
| Assignor returns draft approved or amended | No time limit | Within 4 working days of delivery of draft (LSC 17(1)) |
| Assignee delivers engrossment | Within 3 working days of return of approved draft (NC 19(3)) | At least 5 working days before contractual completion date (LSC 17(2)) |
| Completion | Unless agreed otherwise in the contract 26th working day after later of the date of contract or delivery of the abstract (NC 5(1)) | Unless agreed otherwise in the contract 25th working day after the date of the contract (LSC 21(1)) |
| Completion notice | Once served completion must take place within 16 working days. Time is then of the essence (NC 22(2)) | Once served completion must take place within 15 working days. Time is then of the essence (LSC 23(3)). |

(It should also be noted here that the landlord may not delay granting consent to the assignment or sub-letting unreasonably (1988 Act – see Chapter 6).)

After completion, an application to the Inland Revenue to stamp the deed must be made within thirty days of the date of the document. An application for first registration is made to the Land Registry within two months of completion and for registration of a dealing should be made within thirty working days of an official land registry search to obtain the priority given by that search.

## 2.2 Landlord and Tenant Act 1954, Part II

**Landlord takes the initiative**
Landlord serves s 25 notice given not more than 12, nor less than 6

**Tenant takes the initiative**
Tenant serves s 26 request for a new tenancy beginning on a date

months before the date of termination stated therein, not being earlier than the earliest date on which the current tenancy could have come to an end

Tenant serves counter-notice within 2 months after the giving of the s 25 notice indicating whether or not the tenant will give up possession

specified therein not more than 12, nor less than six months after the making of the request, not being earlier than the earliest date on which the current tenancy could have come to an end

Landlord may serve counter-notice within 2 months of the making of the tenant's request, indicating that it will oppose an application for a new tenancy

Tenant applies to court for a new tenancy not less than 2, nor more than 4 months after the giving of the landlord's s 25 notice or the making of the tenant's s 26 request. The originating application/summons must be served within 2 months and landlord file an answer within 14 days (if county court action)

(See *3.1.3* for a more detailed account.)

## 2.3 Compensation for improvements

After the tenant has served a notice of its intention to carry out certain improvements, the landlord must serve a notice of objection within three months, whereupon the tenant may apply to the court for authority to carry out the works by originating application or originating summons (Landlord and Tenant Act 1927, s 3(1)). At the end of the lease the tenant must make a claim for compensation:

(1) Where the tenancy is terminated by notice to quit within the period of three months beginning on the date on which the notice is given.

(2) Where a fixed term tenancy ends by passage of time, not earlier than six, nor later than three months before the tenancy comes to an end.

(3) Where a fixed term tenancy ends by forfeiture or re-entry within the period of three months beginning with the effective date of the possession order or, if there was no order, within three months of re-entry (1954 Act, s 47).

## 2.4 Leasehold Property Repairs Act 1938

Where there is a lease of any property (save for agricultural holdings) for seven years or more with at least three years to run, then the 1938 Act (as amended by the 1954 Act) stipulates that a landlord before enforcing a right to damages or exercising a right to forfeiture or re-entry must serve a notice on the tenant complying with the LPA 1925, s 146. With regard to a claim for damages, the notice must be served not less than one month before commencement of the action (s 1(2)). If the tenant serves a counter-notice within twenty-eight days, no proceedings for forfeiture or damages can be taken by the landlord without the leave of the court (s 1(3)).

## 2.5 Rent review

Whereas the landlord and the tenant should make every effort to comply with time limits stipulated in the rent review clause, the general rule is that time is not of the essence and therefore the party failing to observe such limits will not be prejudiced. However, there are exceptions to this rule (see *3.2.2*).

## 2.6 Options

There are three main types of option found in a lease:

- to determine the lease known as a break clause,
- to renew,
- to purchase the reversion.

The general rule is that time is of the essence with regard to time limits stipulated in the lease and must therefore be strictly observed (*United Scientific Holdings* v *Burnley Borough Council* [1978] AC 904).

## 2.7 Court fees

Most court proceedings discussed in this book are initiated by originating application or originating summons and thus the fees stated here are confined to the following:

- Issuing an originating application (county court) £30.00.
- Issuing an originating summons (High Court) £60.00.

CHAPTER 3

# STATUTORY RENEWAL AND RENT REVIEW

A good knowledge and understanding of the statutory provisions governing the renewal of business leases and the rules relating to rent reviews are essential for anyone involved in drafting commercial leases. A brief outline of some of the relevant principles is given here, but for a more detailed overview of these areas see TM Aldridge, *Letting Business Premises*, 5th edn (Longman, 1985).

## 3.1 Landlord and Tenant Act 1954, Part II

**3.1.1 Application** A tenant occupying premises for the purposes of business is protected by the Act (s 23(1)). The tenant must occupy some part of the premises and the occupation must be at least partly for business purposes. Business is defined as including a trade profession or employment and any activity carried on by a body of persons (s 23(2)). Various types of occupancy are excluded from the protection of this part of the Act (see in particular s 43(1)) including mining leases, agricultural holdings, tenancies protected by the Rent Act 1977 or the Housing Act 1988, licensed premises (except for hotels and restaurants where a substantial proportion of the business consists of transactions other than the sale of intoxicating liquor, and places of entertainment where the holding of the licence is merely ancillary), and tenancies where the user is in breach of a general prohibition on business use (s 23(4)). Other examples of excluded occupancies are useful to enable the owner to avoid creating a protected business tenancy (see *3.1.8*).

**3.1.2 Effect** Where the tenancy is protected by this part of the Act, termination of the letting can only occur in certain ways:

- by forfeiture of the present or a superior lease;
- by surrender (though an agreement to surrender is void under s 38(1));
- by the tenant holding under a fixed term serving not less than three months' written notice expiring on the date the tenancy would have expired by effluxion of time or on a quarter day thereafter (s 27);
- by service of a landlord's s 25 notice; *or*
- by service of a tenant's s 26 request.

Otherwise, the tenancy will automatically continue beyond the original agreed term on the same terms, save for those inconsistent with such a statutory continuation.

**3.1.3 Procedure** (see also *2.2* and the Precedents in *7.5* and explanatory notes thereto). The landlord should serve a notice on the tenant under s 25 in a prescribed form, stating whether or not the landlord would oppose the tenant's application for a new tenancy and, if so, its statutory ground(s) for possession (see Precedent *7.5.1*). The notice must require the tenant to inform the landlord in writing within two months, whether or not it is willing to give up possession. The notice must be given not more than twelve, nor less than six months before the date it specifies for the termination of the current tenancy. This termination date cannot be earlier than the date when the tenancy would have expired by passage of time or notice to quit given by the landlord. If the tenant wishes to apply for a new tenancy, it must serve on the landlord a counter-notice (for which there is no prescribed form, but see Precedent *7.5.2*) within two months after the giving of the landlord's notice stating that it is not willing to give up possession. The tenant must then apply to court for a new tenancy not less than two, nor more than four months after the giving of the landlord's notice under s 25.

Instead of waiting for the landlord to serve a notice, and provided that the current tenancy is a fixed term exceeding one year or a fixed term followed by a yearly tenancy, the tenant can serve a request for a new tenancy upon the landlord under s 26 in a prescribed form setting out the tenant's proposals for the terms of the new tenancy (see Precedent *7.5.3*). The request must be for a tenancy beginning on a date not more than twelve, nor less than six months after the making of the request, which commencement date must not be earlier than that on which the current tenancy would have expired by passage of time or notice to quit given by the tenant. If the landlord wishes to oppose any application by the tenant to court for a new tenancy, it must serve a counter-notice (for which there is no prescribed form, but see Precedent *7.5.4*), stating that it will oppose such an application and on which statutory ground(s) for possession, within two months of the making of the tenant's request. The tenant must then apply to court for a new tenancy not less than two, nor more than four months after the making of the tenant's request under s 26. Unless the landlord agrees, an application cannot be made outside of these dates (*Kammins Ballrooms Co Ltd* v *Zenith Investments (Torquay) Ltd* [1971] AC 850).

The relevant landlord (known as the competent landlord), for the purpose of the s 25 and s 26 procedure, is the owner of the freehold reversion or of the nearest superior reversion which is not a lease which will terminate within fourteen months by effluxion of time, or because a notice to terminate the tenancy has been served (s 44 and Sched 6). In other words, a landlord whose own lease is coming to an end within fourteen months, drops out of the picture.

Service of notices is as provided by s 23 of the 1927 Act (s 66(4), and see *6.2.1*). The time limits are strict (see the summary in *2.2*) and once the landlord has served an s 25 notice, the tenant cannot serve an s 26 request and vice versa (s 26(4)). If the tenant serves a request but does not apply to the court in time, he cannot start again by serving another and the tenancy will end on the date for commencement of the new term stated in the request (*Polyviou* v *Seeley* (1980) 1 WLR 55). Although a tenant may wish to rely upon a 'continuation' tenancy with its out-of-date rent, there can be an advantage to the tenant in serving an s 26 request for a tenancy twelve months hence, where the landlord has delayed and is about to serve an s 25 notice with a termination date less than twelve months hence. This tactical manoeuvre will delay the commencement of a new tenancy with its revised rent. It will usually be to the landlord's advantage to serve an s 25 notice at the first possible time.

**3.1.4 The court application** In the county court this is by originating application (see CCR Ord 43 and Precedent *7.5.6*) and in the High Court by originating summons (see RSC Ord 97) and, in either case, must be served within two months of issue. In the county court, the matter is usually adjourned generally with liberty to either party to apply to have a day fixed for the hearing (CCR Ord 13, r 3). In the county court the respondent must file an answer (see Precedent *7.5.7*) within fourteen days (CCR Ord 9, r 18(3)).

If the action is brought in the High Court again, rather than have a fixed day for the hearing of the summons, the tenant may request that this be on a day to be fixed. In that court, not less than 14 days before the date fixed for the first hearing of the summons, the tenant must file an affidavit verifying the statement of facts made in the summons (RSC Ord 97, r 7(1)) and, not less than four days before the hearing date, the landlord must serve an affidavit stating whether:

(1) it opposes the granting of a new tenancy and, if so, on what s 30 ground(s);
(2) if a new tenancy is granted, it objects to the tenant's proposed new terms and, if so, which, and the landlord's counter-proposals with regard to the terms;
(3) it has less than 14 years unexpired on its own lease at the date of termination of the plaintiff's current tenancy and, if so, the name and address of its immediate landlord (RSC Ord 97, r 7(2)).

The tenant's application should be registered as a pending land action by a land charge or by a caution at the District Land Registry (as relevant) on the basis that a forfeiture action is so registrable (*Selim Ltd* v *Bickenhall*

*Engineering Ltd* [1981] 1 WLR 1318). The tenant can make an Index Map Search at HM Land Registry to ascertain if the landlord's title is registered and, if so, the title number.

In the majority of cases, the terms of a new tenancy are agreed prior to there being a court hearing. The terms of this agreement can then either be enshrined in a court order (for the county court registrar's powers to make such an order on the day fixed for the hearing see CCR Ord 43, r 15(1)) or, more simply, the tenant can withdraw the application on the agreed terms (see CCR Ord 18, r 1 and Precedent *7.5.8* for notice of discontinuance in the county court). In the High Court leave is required for withdrawal (RSC Ord 21, r 3(1)). Formal withdrawal has the advantage to the landlord of ending the tenancy on a certain date three months following the date of withdrawal (s 64). It is also important that the question of costs be considered and this will normally be dealt with by agreement.

**3.1.5 Grounds for possession** Of the seven grounds summarised below (a) (b) (c) and (e) are discretionary (s 30(1)):

(a) Failure to repair.

(b) Persistent delay in paying rent.

(c) Substantial breaches of other tenancy obligations.

(d) Provision of suitable alternative premises.

(e) The premises form part of property comprised in a superior tenancy and the aggregate rents reasonably obtainable on separate lettings would be substantially less than that reasonably obtainable on a letting of the property as a whole and the landlord requires possession for that purpose.

(f) On termination of the current tenancy the landlord intends to demolish or reconstruct the premises or a substantial part of the premises, or to carry out substantial works of construction on at least part of the premises and could not reasonably do so without obtaining possession. The landlord must prove that it has this intention at the date of the hearing (*Betty's Cafes Ltd* v *Phillips Furnishing Stores Ltd* [1959] AC 20). Where the landlord could carry out the proposed work with possession of part only, or by being given access to and other facilities over the premises then, if the tenant agrees, possession can be ordered on that basis and the landlord will not get possession of the whole premises. The landlord cannot use this ground where the right to enter to carry out the works has been reserved and legal possession (rather than physical possession) is not therefore needed (*Heath* v *Drown* [1973] AC 495 and *Price* v *Esso Petroleum Co Ltd* [1980] 255 EG 243) save perhaps where the works are so substantial that the tenant cannot afterwards operate the business permitted under the lease

(*Leathwoods Ltd* v *Total Oil (Great Britain) Ltd* [1984] 270 EG 1083). See *4.3* for the drafting implications of *Heath* v *Drown*.

(g) On the termination of the current tenancy, the landlord intends to occupy the premises wholly or partly as his residence, or for the purposes of a business to be carried on by it or by a company which it controls. As with ground (f) this intention must be shown to exist at the date of the hearing. This ground is unavailable where the landlord's interest was purchased or created within five years of the end of the tenancy. The current tenancy ends on the date of termination stated in the landlord's s 25 notice or the date of commencement of a new tenancy stated in the tenant's s 26 request. Where the landlord is delaying in order to rely on this ground, until it has been a landlord by purchase for five years, an astute tenant can serve an s 26 request and thereby obtain a new tenancy.

**3.1.6 Compensation** The landlord must compensate the tenant for its failure to obtain a new tenancy where this is solely because the landlord has established one or more of grounds (e) (f) or (g) (s 37). Compensation will be three times the rateable value, or double this sum, where the tenant or its business predecessors have been in occupation for at least fourteen years. The usual provision in a lease that the tenant shall not be entitled to such compensation, is effective where the period of business occupation will be less than five years when the tenant is obliged to leave. The occupation of the tenant's predecessors is included for this purpose, provided that the same business has been carried on in the premises (s 38(2)).

Compensation may also be available for the tenant's voluntary improvements, no matter what the ground for possession under the Landlord and Tenant Act 1927 (see *2.3*).

**3.1.7 New terms** This will often be the only issue between the parties who will serve notices and apply to court merely to protect their respective positions. The Act provides that the terms will be as agreed or:

(1) The premises will be generally that part currently occupied by the tenant known as the holding (ss 23(3) and 32). Thus a tenant who intends sub-letting part of, or the whole of the premises should be first advised of the effect that this can have on renewal.

(2) The duration of the term will be up to a maximum of fourteen years (s 33). Factors such as the length of the previous tenancy (*Betty's Cafes Ltd* v *Phillips Furnishing Stores Ltd*) and the balance of hardship and relative bargaining positions will be taken into account (*Amika Motors Ltd* v *Colebrook Holdings Ltd* [1981] 259 EG 718). Where the premises are ripe for future development the court may be persuaded by the landlord to grant short term or to order a new tenancy containing a

break clause (see cases such as *Reohorn* v *Barry Corporation* [1956] 2 All ER 742, *Adams* v *Green* [1978] 247 EG 49 and the Amika case).

(3) The rent will be the open market rent disregarding the effect on the rent of: the tenant's occupation; goodwill of the tenant's business; improvements made voluntarily by the tenant or during the last twenty-one years; *and* the benefit of any licence where the premises are licensed.

The court can provide for the rent to be reviewed during the term even where there is no rent review clause in the current lease (s 34).

As the new tenancy will not commence until three months after the application has been determined by the court (s 64), the landlord should apply to the court for an interim rent to be fixed once the s 25 notice or s 26 request has been served. This will operate from the date of termination or commencement stated in the s 25 notice or s 26 request, or from commencement of interim rent proceedings if later (s 24A). The application is usually made (in county court proceedings) in the landlord's answer (see Precedent 7.5.7). The landlord can, when drafting the lease, avoid the need for such an application by providing that there shall be a rent review near to the end of the original term (often one day prior to that date).

(4) In fixing terms other than as to duration and rent, the court shall have regard to the terms of the current tenancy and to all relevant circumstances (s 35). In *O'May* v *City of London Real Property Company* [1983] 2 AC 726, HL, it was held that the onus is on the party proposing a change in the original terms to show that it is fair and reasonable. Thus, the tenant should resist the imposition of new more onerous terms such as changing the basis of repairing obligations so that the financial burden falls on the tenant. The tenant on a statutory renewal is therefore in a much stronger position than a new tenant negotiating the terms of a lease. Clearly a tenant, who as a last resort can require the court to determine the terms of the renewed lease, cannot accept any suggestion from the landlord that there can be no amendments to the draft lease to ensure conformity with other lettings in the same building to new tenants (or for some other reason).

**3.1.8 Avoidance** A landlord may wish to avoid the Act and whether the tenant co-operates is a matter for negotiation. There are various methods and the main ones are:

(1) By granting a licence to the occupier. For a discussion of the distinction between a lease and a licence in the light of the leading case of *Street* v *Mountford* [1985] AC 809, HL, see Colbey (op cit). Save in exceptional situations where the occupier has exclusive possession, there will be a lease no matter what the agreement is labelled. Unless the occupier genuinely has no exclusive possession (eg where a supermarket grants a

'concession' to a newsagent to operate in a part of the store and reserves the right to move the newsagent to a different area), the safest approach is not to attempt to create a licence.

(2) By creating a tenancy at will it being held in *Hagee (London) Ltd* v *Ericson (AB) and Larson* [1976] QB 209. This arises where a tenant occupies land as a tenant with the landlord's consent on the basis that either party can bring the tenancy to an end at any time. The danger for the landlord is that regular payments of rent may show that the real intention was to create a periodic tenancy which would be protected by the 1954 Act. Perhaps the best approach is to have a written document stating that a tenancy at will is created and providing for rent to accrue on a daily basis and to be payable at any time when demanded (see Precedent 7.*3*). A tenancy at will is especially useful as a stopgap measure to enable the tenant to enter into possession pending the court's approval being obtained to a fixed term tenancy excluded from the Act's protection.

(3) A fixed term tenancy not exceeding six months, provided that there is no term allowing for renewal beyond this period (s 43(3)). In any event, the tenant and any business predecessor must not have together been in occupation for more than twelve months. Obviously this method is only useful for a temporary short-term letting.

(4) A fixed term tenancy where the parties agree that the 1954 Act will not apply and the court, on a joint application being made, authorises this agreement before the tenancy is created (s 38(4) and see *Essexcrest Ltd* v *Evenlex Ltd* [1988] 1 EGLR). This is usually the best method of avoiding the Act. Approval in most cases is readily obtained, although the parties should be independently advised (see Precedents in 7.*4*). Agreements which purport to preclude the tenant from renewing a business lease are void where the court's approval has not been obtained (s 38(1)).

## 3.2 Rent review

**3.2.1 Purpose** The purpose of rent review is simply to enable the landlord to grant a term of over say three years, while at the same time avoiding being tied to a rent which no longer reflects the level achievable in the open market. Thus a lease will provide that the rent should be reviewed (usually upwards only) at intervals commonly of three or five years. The increase may be made automatic by fixing it to an index. This drafting approach is not recommended as rental values may increase in the open market at a different rate to such an index. The usual method is to provide for rent to be reviewed at intervals to the current open market rent and this type of clause will be the one dealt with in this book (see Precedent 7.*1*).

**3.2.2 Machinery** Early examples of review clauses contain provision for initiating the review by service of a 'trigger' notice by the landlord, for the reaching of agreement between the parties and finally for the appointment of an arbitrator or expert to determine the rent in the absence of agreement, with each stage being governed by time limits. The modern approach is to dispense with a trigger notice and to eliminate time limits as much as possible. Thus the Law Society and RICS have combined to publish a draft model form of review clause in which it is stated that the rent may be agreed at any time between the parties, but in the absence of agreement it will be fixed not earlier than the relevant review date by an arbitrator or expert agreed by the parties or nominated by the President of the RICS on the application of the landlord or the tenant not earlier than six months before the review date, and not later than the end of the review period. Precedent *7.1* uses a similar approach.

Where time limits are stipulated, the general rule is that time is not of the essence (*United Scientific Holdings Ltd* v *Burnley Borough Council* [1978] AC 904). Thus a party who fails to observe a time limit will not be prejudiced by its tardiness either in losing the right to review or to object to the other side's figure and, when the reviewed rent is fixed, will be able to recover it retrospectively (but only with interest if the lease so provides). There are certain exceptions to this general rule:

(1) It is stated in the lease that time is of the essence.
(2) There are other indications in the lease that time limits are strict. Thus the lease may stipulate a time limit and state 'but not otherwise' (*Drebbond* v *Horsham DC* [1978] 37 P&CR 237) or may be structured so that at each stage a certain consequence is deemed to flow from a failure to observe a time limit (*Henry Smith's Charity Trustees* v *AWADA Trading and Promotion Services Ltd* [1983] 47 P&CR 607). However, subtle differences in the drafting of the lease can lead to a different conclusion and this is, in consequence, the most difficult exception to apply.
(3) The presence of a break clause (of which time limits are strict as a general rule) allowing the tenant to terminate the lease by serving a notice to quit after receiving a rent review notice. (*Al Saloom* v *Shirley James Travel Services* [1981] P&CR 81).

It is because of the difficulties which have arisen in practice, that time limits in modern rent review clauses have been reduced to the absolute minimum. Nevertheless, many old business leases are still in existence and both landlords and tenants will often need advice on the effect of the review clauses found in them. Practitioners will sometimes be involved in drafting landlord's trigger notices (see Precedent *7.2*) and tenant's counter-notices which is a process of critical importance where time is, in fact, of the essence. On the renewal of such old leases, the landlord should take the opportunity of updating the rent review clause (1954 Act, s 34(3)).

There should always be a provision for the rent to be fixed by a surveyor in default of agreement the actual person to be as agreed between the parties or otherwise as appointed by the President of the Royal Institution of Chartered Surveyors (the RICS). The address and telephone number of the RICS are 12 Great George Street, Parliament Square, London SW1P 3AD, 01–222 7000. The lease will state whether the surveyor appointed is to act as an arbitrator or an expert. An arbitration will be controlled by the Arbitration Acts 1950 and 1979, which provides for applications and appeals to the court on a point of law. In contrast, an expert's decision is final. Unlike an expert, an arbitrator is obliged to hear evidence and submissions from each party and is bound to reach a decision solely on the evidence presented. Only an arbitrator can order discovery of documents, attendance of witnesses and costs.

Arbitration should be the first choice of the person drafting the lease where rental income will be high, where the building is unusual, or where points of law may be involved. A surveyor may prefer to act as an arbitrator, as only then is he immune from an action in negligence. Appointment of an expert should be considered where the reviews are likely to be straightforward, and quick and conclusive decisions are required.

**3.2.3 Interpretation** Solicitors involved in drafting business leases must be aware of the effect that their handiwork (whether in the lease generally or in the review clause itself) can have on the rent achieved on review. A rent review clause invariably contains a mixture of assumptions and disregards, and a valuer acting in a rent review must inhabit the hypothetical world thereby created. Thus a solicitor should, in anything but a standard case, consult with the landlord's surveyor at the drafting stage, or at least forward a copy of the draft lease for comment.

A specialist work such as DN Clarke and JE Adams, *Rent Reviews and Variable Rents*, 3rd edn (Longman, 1989) or Chapter 4 of Lewison should be consulted to expand upon the brief outlines stated here. The following points should be noted.

The variety of phrases used as valuation formula such as 'open market rent', 'rack rent' and 'reasonable rent' are capable of different meanings, but usually require an objective assessment of the rent. Thus the term 'reasonable rent' was held in one case to mean not what was reasonable between the parties, but rather the rent at which the premises might reasonably be expected to be let in the open market. Thus where there was no express disregard of tenant's improvements these had to be taken into account in fixing the rent review, however unreasonable this was from the tenant's point of view (*Ponsford* v *HMS Aerosols Ltd* [1979] AC 63 HL).

Despite this, in general, phrases such as 'reasonable rent' and 'fair rent' should be avoided, as they may allow the tenant to introduce personal factors.

The tenant should not accept the rent being reviewed to the 'best rent'. In some circumstances this could be higher than the open market rent, as it allows the valuer to have regard to the fact that certain categories of prospective tenant may be willing to pay more than the market rent.

Most review clauses require the valuer to assume that the premises are available to be let by a willing tenant and therefore that there is a market for the premises which may not be the case where they are functionally obsolete (as in *FR Evans (Leeds) Ltd* v *English Electric Co Ltd* [1977] 36 P&CR 185). In such circumstances, the tenant may wish to amend this aspect of the review clause.

The express disregards usually follow those contained in s 34 of the 1954 Act, but should be adapted and set out in full. The practice of incorporating this section by reference has been criticised (*Brett* v *Brett Essex Golf Club Ltd* [1986] 278 EG 1476) and can lead to uncertainty.

One of the most important disregards is that of tenant's voluntary improvements. The tenant should ensure that this disregard covers pre-lease improvements where relevant (see the *Brett Essex* case cited above).

A tenant often obtains a rent free 'fitting out' period at the beginning of a lease to enable it to adapt the premises to its particular requirements. This factor can have the effect of depressing the rent on review and, if the landlord wishes to avoid this possibility, the lease should expressly disregard the fact (as in Precedent 7.*1*) that a rent free period might be agreed on a grant at the relevant review date (see *99 Bishopgate Ltd* v *Prudential Assurance Co Ltd* [1985] 273 EG 984).

The tenant must be careful to ensure that the review clause does not require the valuer to disregard the fact that there are rent reviews. Thus the rent on a ten-year lease without rent reviews would be higher than the rent at the commencement of such a term with a review after say five years. The Law Society/RICS model clause avoids any potential problems in this regard by providing that the rent be assessed, 'subject to the terms of this lease (other than the amount of the rent hereby reserved but including the provisions for review of that rent)' (see also Precedent 7.*1*). There would be potential uncertainty (though probably resolved in the tenant's favour following *British Gas Corporation* v *Universities Superannuation Scheme* [1986] 1 WLR 398) if the rent were instead to be fixed 'subject to the terms of this lease (other than those relating to rent)'.

The estate management advantages of a narrow user clause can be outweighed by its depreciatory effect on rent review and the valuer should take no account of the fact that the landlord may allow different uses unless the user restriction is a qualified one with an express reasonableness proviso (see *Plinth* v *Mott Hay & Anderson* [1979] 38 P&CR 361 and *Forte* v

*General Accident Life Assurance Ltd* [1986] 279 EG 1227). A landlord may provide a narrow restriction on user, but state that a different, more profitable user is to be assumed for the purpose of rent review. The drafter of such a clause should expressly provide that the premises are assumed to be fit for the hypothetical user and that such user is lawful. The tenant should resist hypothetical user provisions if possible.

Although a review clause will normally provide that vacant possession is to be assumed, where there are to be sub-lettings both sides should consider whether or not such an assumption is in their best interests from a valuation point of view. The lack of such an assumption may lead to uncertainty.

There should be an express assumption that the tenant has observed all of its obligations (though this would probably be implied as in *Harmsworth Pension Fund Trustees Ltd* v *Charringtons Industrial Holdings Ltd* [1985] 49 P&CR 297) to make it absolutely clear that the tenant cannot benefit from its own breaches of covenant (see Precedent 7.*1*).

Generally, rental values will depreciate as the lease nears its end, though account should be taken of the possibility of it continuing or being renewed under the 1954 Act (see *Secretary of State for the Environment* v *Pivot Properties Ltd* [1980] 256 EG 1176). Thus the landlord may provide in the draft lease that it will be assumed that rent is being assessed for the full original term. The tenant should argue that the actual residue should form the basis of the valuation. A compromise somewhere in the middle will sometimes result (eg the residue of the term or a specified period of years whichever is longer – see Precedent 7.*1*).

Office precedents for leases generally, and review clauses in particular, need frequent revision. For example, solicitors should, on the introduction of the landlord's right to elect to impose VAT upon rents from 1 August 1989 (see *1.7*), consider whether this could have a depreciatory effect on rents. For the tenant who can recover this VAT, the only problem may be one of cash flow whereas, for the exempt or partially exempt tenant, VAT will represent a significant additional burden. Particularly for such exempt tenants, this could have the effect of reducing rents on the basis that such tenants cannot afford the usual rent plus an additional 15 per cent and a surveyor's advice should be sought in specific cases. A landlord may wish to specify in the review clause that it will be assumed (for rent review purposes only) that the landlord cannot charge VAT upon the rent (see Precedent *1.7*). An alternative approach, directed specifically at those parties who are exempt or partially exempt, is for the lease to provide that it will be assumed that every prospective landlord and tenant is able to recover VAT in full and expressly disregarding the taxable status of any party to the lease. The tenant's solicitor should resist such assumptions and disregards being inserted into a draft lease.

CHAPTER 4

# DRAFTING THE LEASE

In this chapter, only a brief commentary on some of the most important parts of a business lease is provided, but no attempt is made for reasons of space to provide a comprehensive list or to provide examples of business leases in Chapter 7. Such precedents can be found in K Lewison, *Drafting Business Leases,* 3rd edn (Longman, 1989).

## 4.1 The preamble

At the beginning of the lease there may be a list of contents, the date, particulars containing details of the parties to the deed and other information which will vary with each letting, a clause defining frequently used terms and an interpretation clause which should state, amongst other things, that headings and marginal notes are to be disregarded. Terms used in one part of the lease only (such as the rent review clause) are more usefully defined at the beginning of the relevant part.

## 4.2 The description

Particular care should be taken with regard to the property description, especially where the lease is of part of a building so that the full extent of repairing obligatons can be determined. The description must deal precisely with both the horizontal and vertical boundaries and expert advice may be needed with regard to the method of construction of the building. There should usually be a professionally drawn plan on such scale as to enable the exact position of the boundaries to be ascertained. If the verbal description is to prevail over the plan then the plan should be expressed to be 'for identification purposes only'. It will usually be more appropriate for the plan to prevail and a phrase such as 'more particularly delineated on the plan' will be used. Both expressions should not be used at the same time as is sometimes achieved in practice! If a list of fixtures and fittings is incorporated into the description, this can be of great assistance for the purposes of rent reviews and to determine the full extent of repairing obligations and the items the tenant can remove at the end of the lease.

## 4.3 Tenant's rights and landlord's exceptions and reservations

The need for easements and similar rights should be considered by both parties' solicitors. The lease will read more easily if use is made of schedules at the end of the lease rather than setting out such rights in detail after the property description.

The tenant will need, not only a right of physical access including perhaps a right to use a lift, but also rights in connection with services. The tenant may require a right of parking, a right to use sanitary facilities, a right of access to neighbouring properties to carry out repairs to the demised premises and rights of light and air. Although such rights will often be implied, the tenant, in the interests of certainty, should require that they be expressly granted. Conversely, the landlord may wish to exclude certain rights such as those relating to light and air by providing that the landlord has an absolute right to develop its neighbouring property.

Although not strictly correct, the words 'exceptions' and 'reservations' are commonly grouped together to describe all easements and other rights which the landlord is to exercise over the demised premises. Such rights are sometimes drafted as covenants by providing that the tenant shall permit the landlord to do something, thereby enabling the landlord to threaten forfeiture if the tenant is obstructive. The rights will be similar to those granted to the tenant, but will also embrace much more far-ranging rights of access to enable the landlord to enter to inspect the condition and state of repair, and to carry out works to the demised and neighbouring premises. The tenant's solicitors should seek amendments to the draft lease, where necessary, to require the landlord to give reasonable notice before exercising such rights of access and to restore the premises where any damage has been caused.

The landlord must consider carefully the extent of a right to carry out works. If drawn too widely then this may operate to the landlord's disadvantage in preventing the landlord from using ground (f) (see *3.1.5*). The landlord should consider as an alternative, providing a break clause allowing the landlord to determine the lease early where the requirements of ground (f) are satisfied. This redevelopment break clause will serve the same purpose as a right of entry but will not prevent the use of ground (f) (see the precedent in Lewison, Chapter 3). Where development is a real possibility the landlord should consider excluding the 1954 Act (see problem 1 in Chapter 8).

The landlord will usually reserve the right to construct and use new pipes wires, etc on the demised premises for the benefit of its neighbouring premises. The landlord should also reserve the right to affix letting or sale boards to the premises near to the end of the term. Where the lease is longer than twenty-one years, the grant of easements to be exercised in the future, such as the right to lay and use pipes should be limited to a perpetuity period not exceeding eighty years (Perpetuities and Accumulations Act 1964, s 1(1)).

## 4.4 Length of the term

The actual date of commencement of the term should be stated by using a phrase such as 'from and including the 24th day of June 1989'. For convenience, the term is often stated to commence on the last rent payment day falling before the date of the lease and the tenant should ensure that the rent is payable from the latter date rather than the earlier payment day.

## 4.5 Rent

The initial rent and whether it is payable in advance or in arrears will be specified. In the absence of any indication, rent will be payable in arrears and most landlords will require it to be paid in advance. Rent is commonly stated to be payable by equal quarterly payments in advance on the usual quarter days, ie 25 March, 24 June, 29 September and 25 December.

If the landlord insures the property or provides services, the premiums and service charges should be reserved as further rents enabling the landlord to forfeit more easily, or to levy distress if payments are not made.

The provisions for reviewing the rent are usually contained in a schedule. This is one of the most important aspects of a lease and is considered separately in Chapter 3.

## 4.6. Tenant's covenants

**4.6.1 To pay rent** Landlords are vulnerable to a tenant deducting the amount of a claim against its landlord from future rent payments. The right to withhold rent should therefore be expressly excluded. The tenant will usually be required to covenant to pay interest on outstanding rent.

The landlord will have the right to charge VAT on rents but may, as an alternative, agree not to do so if the tenant covenants to reimburse the landlord for irrecoverable input tax perhaps by extending the type of indemnity covenant referred to in *4.6.2* (see also *1.7*).

**4.6.2 To pay and indemnify the landlord against rates, taxes, charges and other outgoings imposed upon the premises or their owner or occupier** This would embrace not only matters such as general and water rates, but less obvious items such as road and maintenance charges. For the avoidance of any doubt, the tenant should make an amendment to such a provision to the effect that the covenant does not relate to any tax liability of the landlord in respect of the rent or arising out of any actual dealing in the landlord's reversionary interest.

**4.6.3 Not to assign underlet or part with possession of the premises** (see Chapter 6) In the absence of any restriction, the landlord will lose control over who may occupy the premises. It is common to bar completely the alienation of part of the premises, but to provide that assigning or underletting the whole is permissible with the landlord's prior written consent. This may not be unreasonably withheld or delayed even if this is not expressly stated.

**4.6.4 Not to carry out alterations** (see Chapter 6) This will usually be made permissible with the landlord's prior written consent which may not be unreasonably withheld. A landlord will see some form of restriction as essential to avoid the tenant having a free hand in this regard (subject to the doctrine of waste).

The landlord may permit a qualified covenant but avoid the statutory restrictions upon withholding consent to some extent by barring the tenant from applying for planning permission or carrying out development as defined for planning purposes. The tenant should try to have such a covenant deleted.

**4.6.5 Not to change the user** (see Chapter 6) The landlord's desire to control the user for estate management reasons and to obtain further control over assignments and sub-lettings should be weighed against the depreciatory effect of such a clause on rental values. If the lease permits a variation in the use of the premises with the landlord's consent, the tenant should require that such consent cannot be unreasonably withheld (as this will not be implied). A landlord will not wish to dispense entirely with controls even if this merely involves barring certain undesirable uses, such as the sale of pornography.

**4.6.6 To keep the premises in repair** Most landlords will wish to achieve a clear lease whereby uncertain expenditure (such as that incurred repairing the premises) will be borne by the tenant. Where the demised premises forms part of a building, shopping centre or industrial estate, or some other larger unit, then the landlord will usually covenant to repair the structure and exterior (leaving the tenant with primary responsibility for the interior) and will recover the cost by way of service charge. The tenant should ensure that this obligation extends to the whole building, centre or estate. Even where the premises do not form part of a larger unit, the landlord should reserve the right to carry out repairs where the tenant fails to do so and to recover the cost as rent. The tenant should resist a clause which appears to make it liable for improvements and should seek the exclusion of insured risks.

In the case of an old building, the tenant may seek to limit its obligations by covenanting to keep the premises in the same condition as at the beginning of the lease. A schedule recording such condition should be prepared by a surveyor and attached to the lease. In the case of a new building, the tenant will wish to exclude liability for inherent defects, which term should be defined in the lease.

Whoever is to be responsible for repairs, the lease should provide that liability will cease where rebuilding is unavoidably prevented by outside circumstances, such as an inability to obtain planning permission. Most importantly of all, the landlord and the tenant between them must be responsible for repair of the whole of the premises with no parts remaining where neither party is responsible, or conversely where both the landlord and the tenant are responsible for certain parts of the premises. Uncertainty can arise where the demised premises are inadequately described. (see *4.2*).

**4.6.7 To pay the landlord's expenses incurred first, in taking any action in respect of the tenant's breach of covenant and, secondly, in the granting of the lease.** The first will include the service of notices, as the landlord should not be left out of pocket with regard to such matters. The insertion of the second is a matter for negotiation (see *1.6.1*).

**4.6.8 To give written notice of a dealing with the premises** This is essential for estate management reasons.

**4.6.9 To comply with the landlord's regulations made from time to time** Such a covenant is common, but potentially very disadvantageous to the tenant. The tenant should at least seek that a proviso is added that the regulations cannot override or contradict the provisions of the lease, nor unreasonably restrict the tenant in its use of the premises.

## 4.7 Landlord's covenants

**4.7.1 To give the tenant quiet enjoyment** This covenant is not usually worded to cover dispossession of the tenant by the true owner or by a superior landlord and it will be difficult for the tenant to have it extended to cover such matters. The tenant should, therefore, try to insist upon the landlord providing proof of its title and advise the tenant of the risks if the landlord will not co-operate in this regard (see *1.5.1*).

**4.7.2 To provide services** This should be inserted where the tenant is required to pay for services by way of a service charge (see *4.8*).

**4.7.3 To insure the premises** Leases usually provide for the landlord to insure and for the tenant to reimburse the landlord with regard to the premiums. The tenant should ensure that there is such an obligation (or other satisfactory arrangement), that the policy is adequate as to the amount and the risks covered and that any shortfall has to be made up by the landlord, that the landlord is obliged to use the funds to reinstate the premises, and that the lease provides that rent will cease to be payable until the premises are reinstated. The tenant should also require that the policy be in joint names, or its interest noted on the policy. The former will give the tenant joint control over the spending of the monies and the latter should at least mean that the tenant is informed by the insurers if the policy lapses.

Alternatively, the tenant may be required to insure with an approved company against specified risks to full reinstatement value and to make up any deficiency out of its own money. Landlords will often not accept a rent abatement clause in this situation and the tenant should insure against its obligation to pay rent during a period where the premises are unusable.

Whoever insures the premises, the lease should state who retains the insurance monies if rebuilding or reinstatement proves to be impossible. The landlord may wish to provide that the monies are retained by the landlord, whereas the tenant may argue that the monies be shared in accordance with a stated formula (eg in proportion with the value of their interests).

Insurance is an area of great importance, and both the landlord and the tenant will expect their professional advisers to be assiduous in protecting their respective interests. It is good practice for all of the landlord's and tenant's obligations and rights in this regard to be dealt with in a separate insurance clause. Deficiencies in the insurance arrangements are then more likely to be picked up at the drafting stage and the parties to the lease can more easily find the relevant insurance provisions rather than (as is often the case) having to look at the tenant's covenants, the landlord's covenants and the provisos.

**4.7.4 Not to let or permit or suffer neighbouring properties to be used for a competing business** In the absence of such a provision, a tenant of shop premises could be subjected to detrimental competition without having a remedy against the landlord (see *Port* v *Griffith* [1938] 1 All ER 295).

## 4.8 The service charge

Reference has already been made in this chapter to the concept of a clear lease (see *4.6.6*). Where the premises form part of a building, shopping centre or industrial estate (described in this context as 'the larger unit') and common services will be provided, the landlord will (by using a schedule) list every service it may wish to provide. The landlord may then create a safety net to catch any it has missed by adding that the tenant must pay for any other service not otherwise mentioned, but supplied by the landlord. The tenant should consider the list carefully and try to eliminate items which it may feel are inappropriate, such as the cost of improvements or rectifying inherent defects. From a landlord's point of view, the 'safety net' provision is probably reasonable, but the tenant should safeguard itself with qualifications, such as that the service must benefit the tenant and that it should be a service for which the tenant would reasonably expect to have to pay.

The parties may feel that it is desirable to provide that the tenants contribute to a sinking fund to be available when required to pay for major expenditure, such as lift replacement. This should avoid the tenants having to suffer major fluctuations in payments which may otherwise mean that an assignee immediately has to pay a large sum for an item in respect of which the assignor has had the benefit, but not the cost of replacing. The tenant should ensure that the lease provides that the fund be held by the landlord upon trust for a perpetuity period of say eighty years, thereby preventing the money falling into the hands of creditors on the landlord's insolvency. However, sinking funds can have adverse tax consequences for both the landlord and the tenants and specialist tax advice is needed before such a fund is created.

There are various ways in which each tenant's share of the burden may be calculated. From the landlord's point of view, a fixed percentage (but with provision for the percentage to be revised to accommodate any extension to the premises or to the larger unit) or a formula (perhaps using the floor area or rateable value of the premises in relation to the combined floor areas or rateable values of the larger unit) has the great advantage of certainty and ease of administration. However, some tenants may place a heavier burden upon services than others and the tenant may prefer a more flexible approach, such as that the tenant shall pay a reasonable or fair share with such proportion to be determined by an independent third party.

The landlord will invariably wish to provide that payments be made in advance based on an estimate with any shortfall or overpayment to be paid or repaid once the actual cost for that year has been determined. The lease will usually provide that this final figure should be certified by a surveyor or accountant acting for the landlord. A proviso that the certificate is final on all matters or on matters of law will be void (*Re Davstone Estate Ltd's Leases* [1969] 2 Ch 378). However, there is no problem from the landlord's point of view if the certificate is stated to be final on questions of fact. It is also important that, if the landlord's surveyor or accountant is given a role in determining the appropriate amount, such person must be separate from the landlord or, alternatively, the lease should make it clear that the landlord's employees can fit this description. Otherwise the certificate may be held to be void (*Finchbourne* v *Rodrigues* [1976] 3 All ER 581).

It is in both parties' interests that the landlord covenants to provide certain services and states whether others are provided at the landlord's discretion. The absence of such a provision will lead to uncertainty as to whether such an obligation will be implied (see *Duke of Westminster* v *Guild* [1985] QB 688).

## 4.9 Provisos

**4.9.1 Re-entry** The landlord will insert a forfeiture clause into a fixed term lease providing that if the tenant does not pay rent (whether formally demanded or not) or breaches some other covenant or condition or becomes bankrupt or enters into liquidation, then the landlord can take possession of the premises. No such rights of forfeiture will be implied.

The proviso for re-entry on the tenant's bankruptcy or liquidation will inhibit the use of the lease as security for a loan and the tenant should try to have this part of the forfeiture clause deleted. The tenant's chances of achieving this are low, save where the lease is at a premium and a low rent, or is otherwise for a long term.

**4.9.2 Suspension of rent** The tenant should insist that the lease contains a proviso that the rent be suspended in circumstances where the premises are unfit for use. The landlord may wish to restrict this to situations where the unfitness arises from destruction and damage by insured risks, save where the cover has been vitiated by the tenant's act, neglect or default. The tenant should insist that the landlord insures against all insurable risks and that the proviso applies also to destruction and damage resulting from risks against which insurance is unavailable or can only be obtained on exceptionally onerous terms. The tenant should try to ensure that the abatement applies also to matters arising outside of the premises, rendering them unusable. It will be a matter for negotiation whether other items commonly reserved as rent (such as insurance premiums and service charge payments) are also to be suspended. The tenant should resist any limitation of the rent abatement to a fixed period of perhaps three years, especially where the landlord has covenanted to reinstate the premises. Otherwise, after this period has elapsed, the landlord may lose any incentive to restore the property.

**4.9.3 Frustration** The lease may contain a proviso permitting the tenant (and possibly the landlord) to bring the lease to an end by notice where the premises have been unfit for a certain period of time. Otherwise, the tenant (and landlord) will have to rely upon the doctrine of frustration applying to terminate the lease in such circumstances which would be a matter of some uncertainty (see *National Carriers Ltd* v *Panalpina (Northern)*

Ltd [1981] AC 675). The tenant should insist on such a proviso being inserted into the lease where the landlord has limited the rent abatement to a fixed period.

**4.9.4 Exclusion of compensation** The tenant's right to compensation under the 1954 Act where the landlord has proved certain grounds for possession, can be excluded in essence where the period of business occupation will have been less than five years by the date on which the tenant is to leave the premises (ss 38(2) and (3)). The landlord will not only wish to insert a proviso excluding these rights where the lease is for less than five years, but also where it is for a longer period on the basis that it may still be effective if the landlord operates a break clause or there has been a change in the tenant and type of business during the term.

**4.9.5 Contracting out** An agreement excluding the 1954 Act with the court's consent must be contained in or endorsed on the lease (s 38(4)). This is most conveniently done by a suitably worded proviso, eg:

> Having been authorised in this regard by an order of the Marton on Tyne County Court (No 1234) dated the First day of September made pursuant to a joint application by the Landlord and the Tenant under the Landlord and Tenant Act 1954 s 38(4) the Landlord and the Tenant agree that the provisions of the Landlord and Tenant Act 1954 ss 24–28 inclusive shall be excluded in relation to the tenancy created by this Lease.

CHAPTER 5

# PROCEDURAL CHECKLISTS

The following checklists are provided to give practitioners an illustration of the procedural steps to be taken on the grant, assignment and surrender of a business lease. They are not intended to be definitive or comprehensive. It is accepted that other practitioners may take different steps or take the same steps in a different order. Some court procedures are touched upon elsewhere in this book. (See Chapter 7).

## 5.1 Grant of lease

**5.1.1 Taking instructions and other preliminary matters** When *acting for the landlord* the following steps are taken:

(1) Basic details are obtained from the landlord and the agent negotiating the grant, including the identity of the tenant and its solicitor, the address of the property, the term, rent, premium, etc, the whereabouts of the title deeds, and whether the tenant is to pay the landlord's legal (and other) costs. It must be ascertained whether the landlord is satisfied as to the tenant's financial status, or whether references should be requested (these will more commonly be obtained by the estate agent). The landlord should be asked for a plan of the premises sufficient for search purposes and all correspondence relating to the proposed terms of the lease. Suggest that all future written communications should be via yourself to avoid the danger of an enforceable contract coming into existence.

(2) Write to the tenant's solicitor confirming your instructions, enclosing a plan for the purposes of the tenant's searches, stating that all correspondence up to exchange of contracts (if any) or completion by exchange of lease and counterpart is subject to contract and lease, and asking for confirmation that the tenant will pay the landlord's costs (if this is to be the case).

(3) Obtain the deeds and examine them, amongst other things, to check ownership, the property description, easements, covenants, mortgages and other third party rights and any superior leases for restrictions on sub-letting and consider whether it is necessary or appropriate to deduce title or to have a contract. If the landlord's title is registered, obtain office copy entries.

(4) If there is a mortgage, check whether the landlord's power of leasing is restricted and, if so, write to the mortgagee for consent to the proposed lease.
(5) Take the landlord's detailed instructions on the terms of the lease, advising the landlord of the various alternative covenants and other matters which should be covered, perhaps using a standard form of lease as a guide. Advise the landlord that it can remain liable on its covenants throughout the term (even after the disposal of its reversionary interest) and whether it is necessary or appropriate to deduce title (see *1.5.1*) or have a contract (see *1.3.2*). Explain to the landlord the effect of the 1954 Act and obtain instructions as to whether there is to be a contracting out of the security of tenure provisions. Advise the landlord with regard to the tax position including the right to elect to charge VAT on rents and premiums (see *1.7*). Discuss with the landlord whether a schedule of the present condition of the property should be obtained and attached to the lease (see *4.6.6*). Obtain a list of fixtures and fittings from the landlord. Arrange with the landlord for professionally drawn plans to be prepared.
(6) Make a site inspection if this is convenient and likely to be helpful.
(7) Make a full company search against a corporate tenant whose substance is unknown, to ascertain its financial position in relation to its obligations under the proposed lease and discuss with the landlord whether there should be a guarantor or rent deposit.
(8) If the grant is of a sub-lease, check the head lease to see, amongst other things, if it contains terms affecting the proposed underletting such as a user restriction or a requirement that the landlord's consent first be obtained, or even that there is an absolute bar on sub-letting. Ensure that the proposed underletting is for a shorter term than that created by the head lease and advise the landlord that it may lose its right to a new lease of the sub-let parts under the 1954 Act (see *3.1.7*). If the head landlord's consent is required, ascertain its requirements for giving consent and provide details of referees (if required).

When *acting for the tenant* the following steps are taken:

(1) Obtain basic details from the tenant and the agent negotiating the grant, including the identity of the landlord and its solicitor, the address of the property, the term, rent, premium, etc and whether the tenant is to pay the landlord's legal (and other) costs. Ask the tenant to let you have all correspondence relating to the proposed terms of the lease and suggest that all future written communications should be via yourself to avoid the danger of an enforceable contract coming into existence.
(2) Write to the landlord's solicitor stating that all correspondence up to exchange of contracts (if any) or completion by exchange of lease and counterpart is subject to contract and lease, and (if authorised by the tenant) confirm that the tenant will be responsible for the landlord's costs.

(3) Take the tenant's detailed instructions on the terms of the lease, checking any information received from the landlord's solicitor or surveyor negotiating the sale and explain that the tenant will be liable under its covenants throughout the term. Advise the tenant that the landlord's own title should be deduced (see *1.5.1*) and whether there should be a contract (see *1.3.2*). Explain to the tenant the effect of the 1954 Act and obtain instructions as to whether there is to be a contracting out. Advise the tenant with regard to the tax position including the landlord's right to elect to charge VAT on rents and premiums (see *1.7*). Discuss with the tenant whether a schedule of the present condition of the property should be obtained and attached to the lease (see *4.6.6*) and, in any event, advise the tenant of the need for a survey. Ascertain whether a mortgage offer is needed before the tenant exchanges contracts (if relevant) or completes the lease.
(4) Make a site inspection if this is convenient and likely to be helpful.
(5) Make a full company search against a corporate landlord whose substance is unknown and which has significant obligations under the lease to repair or provide other services, and discuss with the tenant whether there should be a guarantor of the landlord's obligations.
(6) If the grant is of a sub-lease, obtain a copy of the head lease from the landlord's solicitor and check the matters in paragraph (8) of the landlord's checklist above (where appropriate). Ascertain if the head landlord will require references before granting a licence to sub-let and request details of referees from the tenant (if required).

**5.1.2 Up to completion** When *acting for the landlord* the following steps are taken:

(1) Draft the lease and obtain the landlord's approval before submitting it to the tenant's solicitor in duplicate. If there is to be a contract, draft and submit this to the tenant's solicitor in duplicate at the same time. The draft lease will be attached to the contract. If title is to be deduced, submit an abstract or epitome back to a good root of title, or (if the title is registered) office copy entries and an authority to inspect the register.
(2) In consultation with the landlord, reply to the list of queries submitted by the tenant's solicitor.
(3) Consider the amendments to the draft lease (and contract) made by the tenant's solicitor and, in consultation with the landlord, re-amend this draft document in green (or other different colour).
(4) If a sub-lease is involved, forward the tenant's references to the head landlord and submit to the tenant's solicitor the draft licence to sub-let prepared by the head landlord's solicitor. Amend or approve the form of licence, have the licence executed by the landlord and the tenant (if required) and exchange parts with the head landlord's solicitor before exchange of contracts or (if there is no contract or if the

contract was entered into conditionally upon the licence being obtained) before completion.

(5) If relevant, send the approved draft lease to the landlord's mortgagee for approval and obtain a letter of consent to the letting before exchange of contracts or (if none) before completion.

(6) Write to the landlord, summarising and advising the landlord with regard to the terms of the lease and confirming advice given orally on various matters. A copy of the final form of lease should be sent to the landlord.

(7) If the tenancy is not to be protected by the security of tenure provisions of the 1954 Act, prepare and make the appropriate joint application and obtain a court order under s 38(4) before there is a binding contract, or exchange contracts conditionally upon the obtaining of the order (see *3.1.8* and Precedents *7.4*).

(8) If relevant, have the contract signed by the landlord and attached draft lease initialled and exchange contracts, receiving an agreed proportion (usually 10 per cent) of any premium payable.

(9) Have the draft lease engrossed in two parts, send the counterpart to the tenant's solicitor to be executed by the tenant and have the lease executed by the landlord in escrow in readiness for completion.

(10) Calculate the first rent payment (usually up to the next quarter day). Send a completion statement to the tenant's solicitor incorporating the first rent payment and (if relevant) the property insurance premium, interim service charge payment, the balance of any premium payable (after taking any deposit paid into account) and the landlord's fees.

(11) Complete by handing over the lease and mortgagee's letter of consent (if applicable) in exchange for the counterpart lease and sum due as per the completion statement. If requested, the landlord's solicitor may mark copies or an abstract of its unregistered title deeds as examined against the originals as agent for the tenant.

When *acting for the tenant* the following steps are taken:

(1) Acknowledge receipt of the draft lease, check that its terms broadly accord with the tenant's instructions and send a copy to the tenant.

(2) Send a form of enquiries to the landlord's solicitor appropriate to the grant of a lease to ascertain information such as the planning history of the premises and details of the property insurance policy. Request details of the landlord's title and copies of all documents referred to in the draft lease. Raise requisitions once title has been deduced, including a request that the landlord's mortgagee's consent be obtained before exchange of contracts or (if none) before completion. If the landlord's title is registered, ask the landlord to deposit its land certificate at the Land Registry on completion and to advise you of the deposit number in order that the lease can be noted.

(3) Request a local search and enquiries of the appropriate district or borough council. If the landlord's title has not been deduced or is unregistered, make an index map search at HM Land Registry. Make other searches as appropriate such as a common land and coal mining searches.
(4) Read the draft lease carefully, making appropriate amendments in red. Discuss and explain the lease in detail with the tenant before making final amendments. If these will be of a fundamental nature, obtaining the landlord's solicitor's agreement to the desired changes before making detailed amendments, may save much wasted effort.
(5) Return one copy of the amended lease to the landlord's solicitor and suggest that it be used as a 'travelling draft'. This may pass to and fro several times before agreement is reached.
(6) If a sub-lease is involved, send the tenant's references to the landlord's solicitor, consider and amend the draft licence to assign, have the engrossed licence executed by the tenant (if required) and return it to the landlord's solicitor duly executed. Ensure that the licence has been granted before exchange of contracts (if relevant), or make exchange conditional.
(7) Consider the replies to enquiries and searches and the draft lease and forward a written report to the tenant. This should summarise and advise the tenant with regard to the terms of the lease and any matters arising from the searches and enquiries and confirm advice given orally on various matters. A copy of the final form of lease should be sent to the tenant. The report should re-iterate that the tenant will remain liable throughout the term, even if the tenant sub-lets or assigns.
(8) Check the details of the property insurance and ensure that this will be in force by the time contracts are exchanged or the lease completed (if no contract is envisaged).
(9) If relevant, have the contract signed by the tenant and attached draft lease initialled. Send the tenant's part of the contract to the landlord's solicitor with the agreed deposit once you and the tenant are satisfied that everything is in order including the financial arrangements.
(10) Final searches should be made. A search at the Companies Registry against a corporate landlord where the land is unregistered will ascertain whether there are any floating or fixed charges (pre-1970 fixed charges are binding, even if not registered under the Land Charges Act 1972) and, in the case of registered or unregistered land, will ensure that no resolution to put the company into voluntary liquidation has been passed and that it has not been removed from the register. Full land charges searches should be made against the name of the landlord and previous estate owners or, if appropriate, a registered land search made from the date of office copy entries supplied.

(11) When the engrossed counterpart lease is received, check this against the amended draft lease and have it executed by the tenant in escrow.
(12) Check the completion statement received from the landlord's solicitor and obtain the balance required to complete from the tenant.
(13) Complete the lease as in the landlord's checklist para (11) (*5.1.2*).

**5.1.3 Post-completion steps** When *acting for the landlord* the following steps are taken:

(1) Pay fifty pence stamp duty upon the counterpart lease.
(2) Pay the estate agent's bill if authorised by the landlord.
(3) Account to the landlord for the premium, first rent payment and any other monies received.
(4) If a sub-letting is involved, give notice of the underlease to the head landlord and retain a receipted copy notice with the underlease.
(5) Arrange for the tenant's interest to be noted on the landlord's insurance policy if requested by the tenant.
(6) If appropriate and not attended to before completion, lodge the land certificate at the Land Registry to enable the tenant to note its interest.
(7) Lodge the counterpart lease with the deeds or otherwise in accordance with the landlord's wishes.

When *acting for the tenant* the following steps are taken:

(1) If the title is unregistered, protect an option to renew or purchase the reversion by registration of a C(iv) land charge against the landlord's name.
(2) Pay *ad valorem* stamp duty on the lease within 30 days of completion calculated on the amount of the premium and rent. The rate depends also on the length of the term. Where there is an agreement for a lease, duty is paid on the agreement. Where the lease is for seven years or more, particulars must be delivered within the same time period (Finance Act 1931, s 28).
(3) Give notice to the landlord of any mortgage of the lease entered into by the tenant and retain a receipted copy notice with the lease.
(4) If the lease is for more than 21 years in an area of compulsory registration, apply for first registration within two months of completion. If the title to the reversion is registered, leases granted for more than 21 years must be registered, with a separate title. To preserve priority, this should be done within thirty working days of the registered land search, and also the lease must be noted on the Charges Register of the landlord's title. The Registrar should be reminded to protect an option to renew or purchase the reversion by entry of a separate notice on the landlord's title (though this will usually be done automatically).
(5) Send the lease and other deeds to the tenant's mortgagee and send copies to the tenant. If there is no mortgage, send the deeds to the client or elsewhere in accordance with its instructions.

## 5.2 Assignment of lease

**5.2.1 Taking instructions and other preliminary matters** When *acting for the assignor* the following steps are taken:

(1) Obtain basic details from the assignor and the agent negotiating the assignment, including the identity of the assignee and its solicitor, the whereabouts of the title deeds and whether the tenant is to pay all the landlord's legal costs and/or those incurred in obtaining the licence to assign. If the assignor is also assigning the goodwill of the business carried on from the premises and the fixtures and fittings, ask it to discuss with its accountant the appropriate apportionment between the leasehold estate, the goodwill and the fixtures and fittings and to provide a list of the latter. Ask the assignor to let you have a plan of the premises, the receipt for the last rent payment and details and receipts for service or maintenance charge payments and all correspondence relating to the proposed assignment. Suggest that all future written communications should be via yourself to avoid the danger of an enforceable contract coming into existence.
(2) Write to the assignee's solicitor confirming your instructions, enclosing a plan for the purposes of the assignee's searches, stating that all correspondence up to formal exchange of contracts is subject to contract and seeking confirmation that the assignee is responsible for your costs (if this is the case).
(3) Obtain the title deeds and examine them to check the lease and superior titles, amongst other things, for restrictions on assignment and change of use, the property description and the existence of mortgages and consider to what extent it is necessary or appropriate to deduce superior titles (see *1.5.2*). If the assignor's title is registered, obtain office copy entries of the register.
(4) Ascertain the landlord's requirements with regard to giving consent to the assignment (if relevant).
(5) Take the assignor's detailed instructions with regard to the terms of the contract, including apportionments where the goodwill is also to be assigned. Ascertain whether there are any rent arrears or other breach of covenant, especially relating to repairs. Advise the assignor that, although the contract and assignment will exclude liability for disrepair, this may still be a matter for negotiation, especially if the landlord refuses to give consent to the assignment unless satisfactory arrangements to deal with breaches of covenant are made. Explain that where the assignor has paid a service charge in advance on the basis of estimated figures that the apportionment made on completion can only be provisional. LSC 19(6)(*b*) and NC 6(5) provide that the assignor or assignee will pay any balance or excess due when the actual amount is ascertained. The assignor or assignee may want the contract to make

provision for a sum to be put aside to cover this or for some other arrangements to be made.

Advise the assignor of the importance of investigating the financial standing of the assignee, as the assignor may still be liable for future breaches of covenant. In some cases, a rental deposit may be appropriate. Explain the tax implications of the assignment. Ascertain the approximate amount owing on any mortgages and ensure that there is sufficient to redeem them.

(6) Make a full company search against a corporate assignee whose substance is unknown, to ascertain its financial position and ask the assignee's solicitors for referees or references whether or not required by the landlord in connection with giving consent to the assignment.

When *acting for the assignee* the following steps are taken:

(1) Obtain basic details from the assignee and the agent negotiating the assignment including the identity of the assignee and its solicitor and whether the assignee is to pay all of the assignor's legal costs and/or those incurred in obtaining the licence to assign. Ask the assignee for all correspondence relating to the proposed assignment and suggest that all future written communications should be via yourself to avoid the danger of an enforceable contract coming into existence.
(2) Write to the assignor's solicitor stating that all correspondence up to formal exchange of contracts is subject to contract and (if authorised by the assignee) confirming for what costs the assignee will be responsible.
(3) Take the assignee's detailed instructions and advise the assignee on similar (but not identical) matters to those in para (5) of the assignor's checklist (*5.2.1*) and para (3) of the tenant's checklist (*5.1.1*).
(4) Make a site inspection if this is convenient and likely to be helpful.
(5) Provide details of referees or references to the assignor's solicitor.
(6) Make a full company search against a corporate landlord whose substance is unknown, to ascertain its financial position in relation to its obligations under the lease.

**5.2.2 Up to completion** When *acting for the assignor* the following steps are taken:

(1) Draft the contract and submit it to the assignee's solicitor in duplicate, together a copy of the lease and assignments back to a good root, or (if title is registered) a copy of the lease, office copy entries of the register and an authority to inspect the register together with (whether or not the leasehold title is registered) evidence of superior titles (if these are to be deduced).
(2) In consultation with the assignor, reply to the list of queries submitted by the assignee's solicitor.
(3) Forward the assignee's references or other information required to the landlord and submit to the assignee's solicitor the draft licence to assign

prepared by the landlord's solicitor. Amend or approve the form of licence, have the licence executed by the assignor and the assignee (if required) and exchange parts with the landlord's solicitor before exchange of contracts or completion if the contract was entered into conditionally upon the licence being completed.

(4) Agree the form of contract with the assignee's solicitor, have one part of the approved contract signed on behalf of the assignor and exchange contracts receiving an agreed proportion (usually 10 per cent) of the consideration.

(5) If the full title to which the assignee is entitled was not disclosed before exchange of contracts, forward an epitome/abstract or office copy entries and an authority to inspect the register to the assignee's solicitor.

(6) Reply to any requisitions on title raised by the assignee's solicitor and return one copy of the draft assignments of the leasehold estate and goodwill (if applicable) approved or amended.

(7) Obtain a redemption figure from any mortgagee holding a charge over the leasehold estate and obtain a letter of non-crystallisation from the chargee with regard to a floating charge.

(8) Calculate apportionments of rent and service charge payments from the completion date until the next payment dates and possibly general and water rates and an interim payment for stock (if relevant) pending a final valuation on the day of completion and send a completion statement to the assignee's solicitor requiring payment of the above, any fees agreed to be paid such as the landlord's solicitors and the balance of the price after taking into account any deposit paid.

(9) Have the engrossed assignment executed by the assignor in escrow.

(10) The assignment is completed by handing over the lease, assignment, land certificate or other unregistered title deeds, licence to assign, letter of non-crystallisation (if there is a floating charge) and an undertaking to redeem any charges in exchange for the sum due as per the completion statement. If relevant, give the appropriate sum to the mortgagee to redeem a charge.

When *acting for the assignee* the following steps are taken:

(1) Consider the draft contract, lease and other title details supplied and send a list of enquiries to the assignor's solicitor including a request for a full disclosure of superior titles.

(2) Request a local search and enquiries of the appropriate district or borough council. Make an index map search at HM Land Registry and land charges search against the names of estate owners disclosed whether in connection with the assignor's title or superior titles (if such titles are unregistered). Make other searches as appropriate, including common land and coal mining searches.

(3) Discuss and explain to the assignee the contract, lease and draft licence to assign (in particular that the licence is so drafted as to make the assignee liable throughout the term – see *6.2.2*) and all information obtained from your investigations, enquiries and searches.
(4) Return one part of the contract and the draft licence to the assignor's solicitor either approved as drawn or subject to amendments made to the drafts. If the lease contains fundamental defects then it may be appropriate to insist that the assignor negotiates amendments with the landlord before proceeding.
(5) Forward a written report to the assignee summarising and advising the assignee with regard to the matters discussed and explained as mentioned in (3) above, and confirming advice giving orally. A copy of the lease should be sent to the assignee.
(6) Check the insurance arrangements to ensure that the assignee will be protected from exchange of contracts.
(7) Have the licence to assign executed by the assignee (if required) and the contract signed.
(8) If you and the assignee are satisfied that everything is in order, including the financial arrangements, and the licence has been granted, exchange contracts by forwarding the assignee's part of the contract plus a solicitor's client account cheque for the agreed deposit to the assignor's solicitor. If the licence has not yet been completed, exchange must be conditional upon this being obtained.
(9) Consider any further title details supplied, raise requisitions on title and draft the assignments of the leasehold estate and goodwill (if applicable) submitting these to the assignor's solicitor.
(10) Company searches should be made against a corporate landlord and assignor. Full land charges searches should be made against the assignor landlord and previous estate owners not already the subject of searches (if relevant). Make a land registry search from the date of office copy entries supplied where the title is registered.
(11) Have the approved draft assignment(s) engrossed and executed by the assignee and forward these to the assignor's solicitor in escrow for execution by the assignor.
(12) Check the computations contained in the assignor's completion statement and send a statement to the assignee showing the balance required to complete and your own fees and disbursements including those to be incurred, such as registration fees and stamp duty.

To complete the assignment hand over the sum due in exchange for the documents referred to in para (10) of the assignor's checklist.

**5.2.3 Post-completion steps** When *acting for the assignor* the following steps are taken:

(1) Pay the estate agent's bill if authorised by the assignor.
(2) Account to the assignor for the net sale proceeds.

(3) If relevant, have the mortgage deed receipted or Form 53 sealed by the mortgagee and give notice to the landlord. Forward the deed or Form 53 and receipted copy notice to the assignee's solicitor.

When *acting for the assignee* the following steps are taken:

(1) Pay *ad valorem* stamp duty on the assignment and, where the term is for seven years or more, deliver particulars to the Inland Revenue, both within 30 days of completion.
(2) Give notice to the landlord of the assignment of the lease (and mortgage if appropriate) and retain receipted copy notice(s) with the deeds.
(3) If the assignment is of a lease having more than twenty-one years to run in a compulsory area of registration, apply for first registration within two months of completion. If the leasehold title is registered, apply for registration of the dealing within thirty working days of the registered land search to preserve priority.
(4) Send the deeds to the assignee's mortgagee. If there is no mortgagee, send the deeds to the assignee or elsewhere in accordance with its instructions.

## 5.3 Surrender

The procedural steps are here considered from both parties' points of view.

(1) The terms of the surrender are confirmed in correspondence marked 'subject to contract'.
(2) The landlord's solicitor will ask the tenant's solicitor to provide an epitome or abstract of its leasehold title and to confirm that there is no mortgage or charge affecting that title or to supply office copy entries and an authority to inspect the register. The tenant's solicitor should investigate the landlord's title in the same way. Where the landlord's or tenant's legal estates are mortgaged, the mortgagee should be asked to join in as a party to the deed of surrender to give its consent. Alternatively, a mortgage of the lease may be discharged before completion or, in the case of a mortgage of the landlord's reversion, a letter of consent to the surrender may suffice.
(3) If an agreement to surrender is required, then the approval of the court must be obtained on the joint application of the landlord and tenant under the 1954 Act, s 38(4), unless the lease is unprotected by that legislation. Otherwise the agreement is void under s 38(1).
(4) The landlord's solicitor will submit a draft deed of surrender to the tenant's solicitor in duplicate for approval. It is important for the party receiving any consideration that the deed states that VAT is payable on the consideration (see *1.7* and Precedent *7.6*). Once approved, the landlord's solicitor will engross it in duplicate having the counterpart

sealed by the landlord and sending the deed of surrender to the tenant's solicitor for execution by the tenant.

(5) The landlord's solicitor will send a completion statement to the tenant's solicitor detailing the sums due on completion. This will usually involve a premium to be paid to the landlord or tenant and will also show any rent and service charge payments apportioned up to the date of surrender.

(6) Both the landlord's and the tenant's solicitors should make land charges searches and (if relevant) company searches or search the register of title from the date of the office copy entries supplied.

(7) On completion, the landlord will receive the lease and other deeds held by the tenant, together with the deed of surrender executed by the tenant. The tenant will receive the counterpart lease and deed of surrender. The sum stated in the completion statement will be handed over to the landlord or tenant as appropriate.

(8) If the lease is registered, the deed of surrender should take the form of a transfer to the registered proprietor or owner of the superior estate (see Precedent 7.6). An application should be made to register the surrender by forwarding to the Land Registry the land certificate (or charge certificate and evidence of discharge of the charge) relating to the registered lease and the lease and counterpart. Any notice of deposit or caution must be removed. If the superior title is registered, the land certificate relating to that title must be lodged to enable the notice of the lease to be cancelled. If that title is unregistered, then an examined abstract or epitome should be produced to the Registry. The register will be closed and certificate cancelled with regard to the leasehold title. See PJ Timothy, *Wotner's Guide to Land Registry Practice*, 16th edn (Longman, 1987).

(9) If the lease is unregistered but noted on the registered superior title, application for cancellation of the notice will be made in Form 92 accompanied by the land certificate of the superior estate and the deeds relating to the leasehold estate. See *Wotner*.

CHAPTER 6

# LANDLORD'S CONSENT

## 6.1 General

**6.1.1 Absolute or qualified** A covenant precluding assignment and sub-letting (alienation) alterations or a change of user may be expressed as an absolute restriction, or be qualified by requiring the landlord's prior consent. Various statutes, in particular the Landlord and the Tenant Acts of 1927 and 1988, affect the legal position where a tenant seeks the consent of the landlord to any of these matters

| | *Absolute* | *Qualified* |
|---|---|---|
| Alienation | The landlord can refuse consent on any ground whatsoever | The landlord's consent cannot be unreasonably withheld (1927 Act, s 19(1) or delayed (1988 Act, s 1(2)). A fine cannot be required as a condition for giving consent other than reasonable expenses (LPA 1925, s 144) |
| Alterations | The landlord can refuse consent on any ground whatsoever unless the court's consent is obtained under the compensation procedure of the 1927 Act, or the court orders modification of the lease to enable compliance with other statutory obligations | If the alteration is an improvement (from the tenant's point of view), the landlord's consent cannot be unreasonably withheld. As a condition for giving consent, the landlord can require a reasonable sum for damage or diminution to the value of premises or the landlord's neighbouring premises and proper legal and other expenses. The |

| | | |
|---|---|---|
| | | tenant can be required to undertake to reinstate on termination where this is reasonable and the improvement does not add to the letting value (1927 Act, s 19(2)) |
| User | The landlord can refuse consent on any ground whatsoever | The landlord can refuse consent on any ground whatsoever unless it is expressly stated to the contrary. A fine cannot be required for giving consent except where structural alterations are involved. This does not preclude the landlord requiring a reasonable sum and expenses as with a qualified covenant against alterations (1927 Act, s 19(3)) |

**6.1.2 Application to court for declaration** (See Precedent *7.6* and Atkins Court Forms.) Where consent appears to have been refused unreasonably, the best approach is to apply to the county court for a declaration that the consent has been unreasonably withheld and the dealing, improvement or change of use can proceed without it. Application is by originating application (see CCR Ord 43, r 2). Alternatively, an application can be made to the High Court (see RSC Ord 5), but there is little advantage in doing this as the county court has the same jurisdiction whatever the net annual value for rating purposes and notwithstanding that the tenant seeks no other relief (Landlord and Tenant Act 1954, s 53(1) as amended). It is generally inadvisable for the tenant to proceed without a declaration. The tenant may have interpreted the law incorrectly and have to face forfeiture proceedings to resolve the matter.

## 6.2 Assignment and sub-letting

**6.2.1 Seeking consent** The landlord's consent will not be needed where the lease is silent with regard to assignment and underletting. Where the restriction is absolute, the tenant is not precluded from seeking consent but must comply with the landlord's terms, however unreasonable. If the landlord gives consent, there should be a deed of variation amending the lease to permit the dealing.

Most commonly, the restriction is qualified and thus the landlord is constrained by the fact that consent cannot be unreasonably withheld. The tenant will apply for consent (not the prospective assignee or sub-tenant) usually via an agent such as a solicitor or surveyor submitting to the landlord or its agent a bank reference and two trade references relating to the assignee or sub-tenant. The request for the bank reference should be made direct by one bank (commonly the assignor's solicitor's bank) to the assignee's bank. Ideally, the letter requesting the reference should contain details of the financial burden to be faced by the assignee by stating the length of the term, the premium, the rent and whether any rent review is pending and the anticipated cost of the works of conversion or fitting out, or to rectify dilapidations. It is good practice to send this letter to the landlord with the reference. The ideal references will be unqualified and explain why the assignee is suitable.

The landlord can ask for whatever information is reasonable to enable it to ascertain whether the assignee or sub-tenant is suitable such as, in appropriate cases, accounts and profit projections.

A recent Court of Appeal decision, *International Drilling Fluids Ltd* v *Louisville Investments (Uxbridge) Ltd* [1986] 2 WLR 581, reiterated the main principles governing whether a refusal is unreasonable, though these must now be read in the light of the 1988 Act. Amongst other things, it was stated that a landlord is not entitled to refuse consent on grounds having nothing to do with the relationship of landlord and tenant with regard to the subject matter of the lease. For example, it would not be a valid reason that the landlord does not want another service user but wants to force a change to a more profitable user. A landlord will sometimes refuse consent because the premises are dilapidated. However, this will generally only be relevant (except in serious cases) where evidence is unavailable to show that the prospective assignee is ready, able and willing to put the property in repair within a reasonable time (*Orlando Investments Ltd* v *Grosvenor Estate Belgravia* [1988] 49 EG 85). Any conditions imposed by the landlord must be reasonable. Thus, there is no automatic right for the landlord to insist upon guarantors or upon the proposed assignee or sub-tenant joining in the licence to covenant direct with the landlord, even where the lease purports to make these conditions for the giving of consent. See TM Aldridge, *Letting Business Premises*, 5th edn (Longman, 1985) on the question of reasonableness.

The Landlord and Tenant Act 1988 has placed tenants in a much stronger position than hitherto. A landlord served with a written request for consent to a dealing must, within a reasonable time, give consent in writing (unless it is reasonable to withhold it), stating any conditions to which consent is subject and reasons (where relevant) for withholding consent (s 1(2)). The onus is now upon the landlord to show that it has acted reasonably with regard to time, refusing consent or imposing conditions (s 1(6)). Where a superior landlord's consent is also required and may not be unreasonably withheld, the same obligations extend to the superior landlord (s 3). A claim for breach of statutory duty can be made where a person is in breach of its obligations under the Act (s 4). Service of applications or notices under the 1988 Act are as provided in the lease or, where there is no such provision, as provided by s 23 of the 1927 Act (personal service, or left at, or sent by registered post or recorded delivery to the last-known place of abode in England or Wales and, in the case of a notice to a landlord, the person on whom service may be effected includes any duly authorised agent of the landlord). The new legislation probably does not alter the existing law as to what will constitute good reasons for refusing consent save perhaps for the unclear s 1(5) which provides that: 'For the purposes of this Act it is reasonable for a person not to give consent to a proposed transaction only in a case where, if he withheld consent and the tenant completed the transaction, the tenant would be in breach of a covenant' (eg the qualified covenant itself or a user restriction).

Where the lease contains a proviso that before seeking consent the tenant must first offer to surrender, the tenant must go through the ritual of offering to surrender. If the landlord accepts, the agreement to surrender is void where the 1954 Act applies to the tenancy (s 38(1)). The tenant then may seek consent in the normal way (*Allnatt London Properties Ltd* v *Newton* [1984] 1 ALL ER 423).

Often an agreement to assign (or sometimes sub-let) will be entered into conditionally upon consent being obtained (see NCS 11(5) and LSC 8(4)). It is desirable that the licence be obtained before exchange. The National Conditions of Sale do not make it clear by what time consent should be obtained and therefore when rescission can take place (see *29 Equities Ltd* v *Bank Leumi (UK) Ltd* [1986] 1 WLR 1490). A special condition covering such points should be added to the contract where the tenant and prospective assignee wish to commit themselves subject to the licence being obtained.

**6.2.2 Drafting the licence** (see Precedent 7.7) Often, the landlord's solicitor will write to the tenant's solicitor stating that, before any work is done, the tenant's solicitor must undertake to be responsible for the landlord's costs. The tenant's solicitor should only give an undertaking to pay the landlord's reasonable costs after agreeing a maximum figure with the landlord's solicitor with the authorisation of the tenant and (if this can be achieved without embarrassment) after obtaining sufficient money from the tenant on account to cover this figure. Alternatively, the tenant's solicitor should politely decline, again agreeing a maximum figure and confirming, with the tenant's authority, that the tenant will be responsible for reasonable fees up to that figure.

The landlord's solicitor will prepare a draft deed giving consent and will send it in duplicate to the tenant's solicitor who will in turn forward it to the assignee's solicitor. Once approved by all relevant parties, an engrossment will be prepared by the landlord's solicitor. One copy will be executed by the assignee and one by the landlord and the parts exchanged so that the tenant has the landlord's executed part and vice versa. If, as the landlord usually requires, the assignee is to enter into direct covenants with the landlord, then the licence will be in three parts. Sometimes all three parts (or two as the case may be) will be executed by each party. When the licence has been completed each party will hold one part.

In the licence, the landlord will consent to the assignment or sub-letting and the tenant will, amongst other things, covenant to pay the landlord's costs. The assignee may be required to covenant to observe the covenants in the lease during the residue of the term. Without such a covenant an assignee is only liable up until it disposes of its own interest and should resist entering into a covenant in the terms required by the landlord. It is undecided whether such a requirement is justified in the context of an assignment. Similarly, a sub-tenant is not liable to a superior landlord and such a landlord may try to avoid this problem by requiring direct covenants in the licence to underlet. In the post-1988 Act climate tenants should be more ready to challenge landlord's requirements without being so concerned about possible delay.

## 6.3 Alterations

**6.3.1 Seeking consent** If the lease does not expressly forbid the proposed alterations, the tenant does not need to seek the landlord's consent (subject to the doctrine of waste). If the alterations are absolutely forbidden, the tenant can seek consent (which may be given by a deed varying the lease) or refused, however unreasonably.

Whether the restriction on alterations is absolute or qualified, the tenant may obtain the court's consent under the compensation procedures of the 1927 Act (see *2.3*) or otherwise make application to the court where legislation allows the court to modify the lease to enable the tenant to comply with statutory obligations such as those imposed by the Fire Precautions Act 1971 (see Aldridge).

Where there is a qualified covenant precluding alterations except with the landlord's consent then, with regard to improvements, there is an implied reasonableness proviso extending to refusal or consent subject to permitted conditions. The availability of such conditions means that the landlord will rarely be able simply to refuse consent to improvements outright and the issue will often turn on the reasonableness of the conditions.

The landlord should require the fullest possible information with regard to the proposed alterations, including plans and evidence of planning, building regulations and other appropriate consents and approvals.

**6.3.2 Drafting the licence** A draft deed granting consent is prepared by the landlord's solicitor and submitted in duplicate to the tenant's solicitor. When approved, it will be engrossed in duplicate. Generally, one part will be executed by the tenant and one by the landlord. Both parts will be exchanged so that the tenant has the licence executed by the landlord, and the landlord the counterpart executed by the tenant.

The main drafting issues are: first, what conditions the landlord should impose and the tenant accept; and secondly, whether the tenant should be placed under an obligation to carry out the works.

Although the landlord can require the payment of money or reinstatement at the end of the lease, the tenant is only obliged to accept such conditions if they are reasonable. The landlord should consider a reinstatement provision where the alterations are of benefit only to the tenant. Where the improvements add to the letting value, the tenant can resist a reinstatement condition and thereby preserve its rights to compensation under the 1927 Act. Compensation must not exceed the net addition to the value of the premises and if the reinstatement takes place there will be no such addition. Where a reinstatement condition is inserted the landlord should consider attaching both 'before' and 'after' plans. Such plans will also be good evidence for determining the rent on review and statutory renewal under the 1954 Act where improvements are to be disregarded.

Imposing an obligation upon the tenant to execute the works has certain advantages so far as the landlord is concerned.

First, s 2(1) of the 1927 Act provides that compensation is unavailable for improvements carried out by the tenant pursuant to a contract for valuable consideration. Such consideration includes a rent free period, a payment of money to the tenant exceeding a nominal figure (but not necessarily representing full compensation), or possibly even waiving the benefit of an absolute bar on alterations.

Secondly, s 34 of the 1954 Act stipulates that tenant's voluntary improvements should be disregarded in determining the rent on renewal of the lease pursuant to the Act and most rent review clauses are drafted to similar effect. It is extremely disadvantageous to the tenant to pay the actual cost of the improvements and then to have to pay a higher rent, in consequence, on renewal or review.

Care must be taken with regard to drafting. A landlord will wish to require the tenant, amongst other things, to execute the works pursuant to planning and building regulations and other statutory consents and in a good and workmanlike manner. However, the tenant may still have the choice whether to carry out the works in the first instance and thus there may be no obligation involved. Ideally, the licence should expressly state whether or not the tenant is under such an obligation.

## 6.4 User

**6.4.1 Seeking consent** Whether the covenant restricting the user is absolute or permits a change with the landlord's consent, the landlord can refuse consent or impose onerous conditions without constraint save that, where the covenant is qualified, a fine can only be required where the change involves structural alterations. Generally (though note the landlord can in some circumstances require a 'reasonable sum'), a landlord need only act reasonably where a qualified covenant expressly requires it not to refuse consent unreasonably. The circumstances justifying a refusal of consent where there is a reasonableness proviso are similar to those where a landlord can refuse consent reasonably to an assignment or sub-letting.

**6.4.2 Drafting the licence** The procedure involved is similar to that where there is a licence permitting alterations. Where the covenant is absolute, the licence will take the form of a deed varying the user clause. The landlord's solicitor should make consent conditional upon the tenant obtaining planning permission and any other appropriate consents and should also carefully consider the rent review implications. The lease may need to be varied so that the rent on review is the higher of the rental values where the premises are, first, let for the existing user and, secondly, for the new user. However, the amended user clause should then provide that it will be assumed (where appropriate) that the premises have been physically adapted and may lawfully be used for the existing user. Failure to provide such express assumptions may have a depreciatory effect on the rental value of the existing user once planning permission has been obtained and alterations made in connection with the new user. This will be a costly mistake if the new user commands a lower rental value.

CHAPTER 7

# PRECEDENTS

## 7.1 Rent review clause

RESERVATION OF RENT

YIELDING AND PAYING therefore to the Landlord yearly during the Term and in proportion for any less time than a year:

(1) The yearly rent of £10,000 or such other yearly rent as shall be determined in accordance with the provisions of the Fourth Schedule hereto by four equal quarterly payments in advance on the usual quarter days.

(2) By way of further rent ('the Further Rent') . . . (*Note* that this would include matters such as insurance premiums and service charge payments.)

THE FOURTH SCHEDULE

1 In this Schedule the following expressions shall have the following meanings:

(1) 'Review Date' means the Twenty-fifth day of March One thousand nine hundred and ninety four and each fifth anniversary of such date thereafter during the term.

(2) 'Rent' shall not include the Further Rent.

(3) 'Quantified Rent' means the yearly rent of £10,000 reserved and made payable under this Lease.

(4) 'Relevant Review Date' means that Review Date at which the Rent is being agreed or determined pursuant to the provisions of this Schedule.

(5) 'Open Market Rent' means the full yearly market rent at which the Premises might reasonably be expected to be let in the open market with vacant possession on the Relevant Review Date by a willing landlord to a willing tenant without taking a premium

(a) for a term equal to the residue of the term hereby granted or for a term of 10 years (whichever is longer) and on the basis (whether or not it is a fact) that the Premises enjoy planning permission and all other consents and approvals required for the permitted user of the Premises for the time being authorised by the terms of this Lease and also on the basis that there is taken into account the possibility of the tenancy created by this Lease being continued or renewed under the provisions of Part II of the Landlord and Tenant Act 1954 (as amended by the Law of Property Act 1969)

(b) otherwise upon the terms and conditions contained in this Lease (save as to the amount of Rent hereby reserved but including the provisions for rent review herein contained)

(c) on the assumption (whether or not it is a fact and without prejudice to any rights of the Landlord in regard thereto) that

(i) the Tenant has duly complied with all of the covenants on the part of the Tenant contained in this Lease

(ii) all parts of the Premises are fully fitted out and equipped and are immediately available and fit for use for the purposes herein permitted

(iii) the Landlord will give consent to a change of use or assignment or underletting and

(iv) any destruction or damage to the Premises has been fully restored or rectified

(v) Value Added Tax or any similar tax cannot be charged (whether or not at the Landlord's election) upon the rents payable under this Lease

(d) but disregarding

(i) any goodwill attached to the Premises by reason of the carrying on thereon of the trade or business of the Tenant or of any permitted sub-tenant or their respective predecessors in title

(ii) any effect on rent of any improvements (to which the Landlord shall have given written consent) carried out by the Tenant or permitted sub-tenant or their respective predecessors in title other than in pursuance of an obligation to the Landlord or at the expense or partly at the expense of the Landlord

(iii) any effect on rent of the fact that the Tenant or any sub-tenant or their respective predecessors in title may have been in occupation of the Premises and

(iv) any rental concession which might on a new letting be made to an incoming tenant

(6) 'Revised Rent' shall mean the yearly Rent payable in substitution for the Quantified Rent or for a previous revised Rent

(7) 'President' means the President for the time being of the Royal Institute of Chartered Surveyors (or any body for the time being performing its functions as successor to it) or any person for the time being authorised to act on its behalf

2 From and after each Review Date the Rent shall be the Rent agreed in writing between the Landlord and the Tenant or (in the absence of agreement) shall be whichever is the highest of:

(1) the yearly Rent payable in the year ending on that review date ('the Current Rent') and

(2) the Open Market Rent

3 If the Landlord and Tenant shall not have agreed in writing the Open Market Rent by the Relevant Review Date the Landlord or the Tenant may at any time thereafter (but before the Review Date next following the Relevant Review Date) require in writing to the other of them an independent surveyor ('the Surveyor') to determine the Open Market Rent as at the Relevant Review Date.

4 The Surveyor (who shall be a member of the Royal Institution of Chartered Surveyors and be experienced in the valuation of premises of a like nature to the Premises in the area in which the Premises are situated) may be agreed upon by the Landlord and the Tenant and in default of such agreement within two months of a requirement being made pursuant to clause 3 of this Schedule shall be appointed by the President on the application of either the Landlord or the Tenant made at any time after the said period of two months.

5 (1) Unless the Landlord and the Tenant agree to the contrary the Surveyor shall act as an arbitrator and the arbitration shall be conducted in accordance with the Arbitration Acts 1950 and 1979

(2) The Surveyor shall give notice in writing of his decision to the Landlord and the Tenant within four months of his appointment or within such extended period as the Landlord and the Tenant may at any time agree

6 If the Surveyor shall fail to determine the Open Market Rent and to give notice thereof within the time and in manner hereinbefore provided or shall relinquish his appointment or die or otherwise fail or be unable to determine the same the Landlord may apply to the President for a substitute to be appointed in his place which procedure may be repeated as many times as necessary.

7 In the event that by the Relevant Review Date the Landlord and the Tenant shall not have agreed in writing or otherwise ascertained the Revised Rent to be payable from and after such date the Tenant shall continue to pay Rent at the rate of the Current Rent on each day appointed by this Lease for payment of Rent until the quarter day immediately following the ascertainment of the Revised Rent and the difference between the Current Rent and the Revised Rent from the Relevant Review Date until such quarter day shall be added to and be payable with the instalment of the Revised Rent due on such quarter day together with interest thereon calculated from day to day at the rate of four per cent above the Base Lending Rate of Broomleys Bank plc prevailing from time to time for the same period on the amount of such difference.

8 Immediately after the Open Market Rent shall have been agreed or determined as aforesaid and shall result in a Revised Rent a memorandum of such Revised Rent in such form as the Landlord may reasonably require shall be endorsed on or annexed to this Lease and the Counterpart thereof at the expense of the Tenant and the Landlord respectively.

9 For the avoidance of any doubt a Revised Rent shall be payable on the days and in the manner in this Lease appointed for payment of the Quantified Rent and the terms of this Lease relating to the suspension of Rent and the consequences of non-payment shall apply to a Revised Rent in the same manner as to the Quantified Rent.

10 If at any time or times during the continuance of this Lease there shall be in force any Act of Parliament which shall restrict or in any way affect the Landlord's right to payment of a Revised Rent the Landlord shall be entitled following the repeal termination or modification of such Act (but in the event of a modification of such Act only to the extent permitted by such modification) to serve notice upon the Tenant

requiring a review of the Rent as from the first quarter day ('the Interim Review Date') occurring not less than twenty-eight days after the date of service of the Landlord's notice whereupon in the absence of agreement a Surveyor shall be appointed to determine such matter in accordance with the foregoing provisions of this Schedule so far as the same shall be applicable with the substitution of the Interim Review Date for the Relevant Review Date.

*Note*

The landlord's solicitor may consider, in consultation with the landlord's surveyor, adding an express assumption along the lines of clause 1(5)(*c*)(v) to negate any depreciatory effects of the landlord's right to impose Value Added Tax upon the rent (see *1.7* and *3.2.3*).

## 7.2 Rent review trigger notice

**To (Tenant) of (address)**

NOTICE IN CONNECTION WITH RENT REVIEW

| | |
|---|---|
| The Premises: | 13 High Row Marton on tyne |
| The Landlord: | A Limited whose registered office is situated at 1 High Street Worktown |
| The Tenant: | B Limited whose registered office is situated at 10 Sea Road Durton on Sea |
| The Lease: | A lease of the Premises dated 8 April 1984 and made between the Landlord (1) and the Tenant (2) for a term of 15 years commencing on 25 March 1984 at an initial rent of £15,000 per annum |
| The Review Date: | 25 March 1989 |
| The Review Provisions: | The provisions for reviewing the rent at five yearly intervals contained in the Fourth Schedule of the Lease |

As agents for the Landlord we give you notice under the Review Provisions that:

(1) The Landlord requires that the rent of the Premises be reviewed as at the Review Date
(2) The rental of £25,000 per annum is in the opinion of the Landlord the open market rent of the Premises as at the Review Date

Dated:

Signed:

A Solicitor and Co
23 High Street
Worktown

*Note*
A trigger notice is often not required (eg Law Society/RICS Model Clause and Precedent 7.*1*) and does not always have to state the required rent. The review clause should be read carefully and this notice, which is only an illustration, must be adapted to fit the circumstances and to follow the wording of the lease. Thus paras (1) and (2) will often be alternatives. Where time is of the essence the trigger notice is of critical importance as indeed is any counter-notice to be served by the tenant.

## 7.3 Tenancy at will

THIS AGREEMENT is made on the first day of July 1989 BETWEEN A LIMITED whose registered office is 1 High Street Worktown ('the Landlord') of the one part and B LIMITED whose registered office is 10 Sea Road Durton on Sea ('the Tenant') of the other part

WHEREAS:

(1) The Landlord intends ultimately to carry out certain alterations to the premises demised by this agreement and in the meantime wishes to let the premises on a temporary basis

(2) The Tenant wishes to occupy the premises temporarily for the purposes of its business of the sale of fruit and vegetables

(3) The Landlord wishes to grant and the Tenant wishes to take a tenancy at will of the premises

IT IS AGREED as follows

1 The Landlord lets and the Tenant takes the premises known as 10 High

Street Worktown ('the Premises') on a tenancy at will commencing on the 7th day of July 1989

2 The Tenant will pay a rent calculated at the rate of Twenty pounds (£20.00) per day whenever the Landlord shall demand it provided that neither the payment of rent at regular intervals nor the subsequent calculation of rent by reference to a period is intended nor shall give rise to a periodic tenancy

3 The Tenant agrees with the Landlord:

(a) To pay the rent without deduction when demanded

(b) To pay and indemnify the Landlord against all taxes outgoings charges and rates payable in respect of the Premises

(c) Not to make any alterations to the Premises

(d) To keep the Premises in the same state of repair and decorative condition as existed on the commencement date of this tenancy as evidenced in the Schedule of Condition annexed to this agreement

(e) Not to assign underlet charge share or otherwise part with possession of the Premises

(f) Not to use the Premises or any part of the Premises otherwise than for the sale of fruit and vegetables

(g) Not to cause any nuisance or annoyance to the Landlord or to the owner or occupier of any neighbouring premises

(h) To permit the Landlord and all persons authorised by the Landlord to enter the Premises on giving twenty-four hours' notice or at any time in an emergency to inspect or carry out works to the Premises or any neighbouring premises

IN WITNESS whereof the parties hereto have hereunto caused their Common Seals to be affixed the day and year first hereinbefore written

THE COMMON SEAL OF A LIMITED
was hereunto affixed in the presence of:

Director

Secretary

THE COMMON SEAL of B LIMITED
was hereunto affixed in the presence of:

Director

Secretary

*Note*

A tenancy at will is not protected by the Landlord and Tenant Act 1954 Pt II and can be brought to an end at any time by either party without any need for a break clause or proviso for forfeiture. It is desirable to include recitals explaining the circumstances as the tenancy at will must be genuine. The drafter must be careful not to create a periodic tenancy and this has been achieved here by creating a daily rent. Such a tenancy should only be used on a short-term basis as regular payments of rent with reference to a period may give rise to the implication of a periodic tenancy.

## 7.4 Forms in connection with a joint application to the county court for an order under s 38(4) of the Landlord and Tenant Act 1954 Pt II

### 7.4.1 Request for issue of originating application under s 38(4)

IN THE WORKTOWN COUNTY COURT MATTER NO.

BETWEEN:

Walter Smith First Applicant

and

X Limited Second Applicant

We hereby request that the accompanying originating application be issued in accordance with the instructions contained therein.

DATED this First day of August 1989

| ........................................ | ........................................ |
|---|---|
| A Solicitor and Co<br>23 High Street<br>Worktown | Hopitees<br>The Towers<br>Worktown |
| Solicitors for and on behalf of the First Applicant | Solicitors for and on behalf of the Second Applicant |

To the Registrar

### 7.4.2 Originating application under s 38(4)

IN THE WORKTOWN COUNTY COURT MATTER NO.

In the Matter of the Landlord and
Tenant Act 1954

and

In the Matter of a Proposed Lease
of the Premises being
45 High Street Worktown

BETWEEN

Walter Smith — First Applicant Landlord

and

X Limited — Second Applicant Tenant

1 WALTER SMITH of 44 The Avenue Newtown ('the First Applicant') and X LIMITED whose registered office is situate at the Grange Worktown ('the Second Applicant') HEREBY APPLY to the Court for an Order ('the Order') under s 38(4) of the Landlord and Tenant Act 1954 Part 2 as amended ('the Act') authorising the inclusion in a Lease (an agreed draft of which is attached to this application) to be made between the First Applicant of the one part and the Second Applicant of the other part of premises known as 45 High Street Worktown ('the Premises') of an agreement excluding the provisions of ss 24–28 (inclusive) of the Act in relation to the tenancy thereby created.

2 THE grounds upon which the First Applicant and the Second Applicant claim to be entitled to the Order are that first the First Applicant may wish to redevelop the Premises at short notice and that secondly exclusion of the Second Applicant's rights have been taken into account when negotiating the length of term granted and the rent reserved by the proposed Lease.

3 The Second Applicant has received legal advice independently from the First Applicant and is aware of the rights which it would have under the Act but in the circumstances mentioned in the preceding paragraph the Second Applicant considers it reasonable that it should forgo such rights and has therefore agreed to make this Application.

4 The First Applicant and the Second Applicant hereby agree pursuant to s 63(3) of the Landlord and Tenant Act 1954 that this application should be made to the Newtown County Court notwithstanding first that any assessment of rateable value made or to be made in respect of the Premises might otherwise necessitate the hearing of the application in the High Court and that secondly the premises are not within the jurisdiction of the Newtown County Court.

IT IS NOT INTENDED to serve any other person with this Application.

DATED this First day of August One thousand nine hundred and eighty nine.

| .......................................... | .......................................... |
|---|---|
| A Solicitor and Co.<br>23 High Street<br>Worktown | Hopitees<br>The Towers<br>Worktown |
| Solicitors for and on behalf<br>of the First Applicant | Solicitors for and on behalf<br>of the Second Applicant |

TO: THE REGISTRAR OF THE NEWTOWN COUNTY COURT

### 7.4.3 County Court Order excluding the 1954 Act

IN THE WORKTOWN COUNTY COURT MATTER NO

In the Matter of the Landlord and
Tenant Act 1954

and

In the Matter of a Proposed Tenancy
of the Premises Known as
45 High Street Worktown

BETWEEN

Walter Smith First Applicant

and

X Limited Second Applicant

UPON THE JOINT APPLICATION of the First Applicant and the Second Applicant and it appearing that the Applicants jointly apply for the relief sought by this application and by their respective solicitors have consented in writing to this Order.

IT IS ORDERED pursuant to s 38(4) of the Landlord and Tenant Act 1954 that the Applicants be at liberty to enter into an agreement excluding the provisions of ss 24 to 28 inclusive of the said Landlord and Tenant Act, 1954 in relation to the intended tenancy to the Second Applicant such agreement to be in the terms contained in the said intended tenancy agreement a draft whereof is attached to this Order and signed by the Registrar

Dated this day of 1989

REGISTRAR

*Note*

The application is made by joint originating application to the appropriate county court (see Notes to Precedent *7.5.6*). As the county court procedure is easier and quicker, the applicants will normally file the application in the county court even though the rateable value may exceed £5,000 (the county court limit). This may be done by agreement in writing (1954 Act, s 63(3)) which is often contained in the originating application itself (see Precedent *7.4.2*, para 4). The applicants (normally via the landlord's solicitor) will file:

(a) self-addressed envelopes where the application is made through the post
(b) a request
(c) an originating application and two copies with the agreed form of lease attached
(d) a draft court order signed by both parties' solicitors containing a statement that, 'We hereby consent to an order in these terms' and (as a matter of courtesy) three further copies without such a statement for use by the court
(e) a cheque for £30.00

The application may be heard and determined by the registrar in chambers (CCR Ord 43, r 15(2)). It is unusual for either party to attend at court and the application is normally dealt with through the post.

The agreement is usually contained in a proviso in the lease (see *4.9.6*).

# 7.5 Statutory renewal forms

Examples are given of the following:

- 7.5.1: *Landlord's s 25 notice*
- 7.5.2: *Tenant's counter-notice*
- 7.5.3: *Tenant's s 26 request*
- 7.5.4: *Landlord's counter-notice*
- 7.5.5: *Request for originating application in the county court*
- 7.5.6: *Tenant's originating application*
- 7.5.7: *Landlord's answer*
- 7.5.8: *Notice of discontinuance*

It should be noted that *7.5.3* and *7.5.4* are alternatives to *7.5.1* and *7.5.2*. Which is relevant depends upon whether the landlord or the tenant is the first to initiate the 1954 Act procedure by serving a s 25 notice or s 26 request respectively. The advantage often lies with whosoever serves the notice or request (see *3.1.3*). Thus in the examples given, the landlord has delayed serving a s 25 notice which would enable the tenant to extend its tenancy by serving a s 26 request for a new tenancy twelve months hence (before the landlord serves its s 25 notice to terminate the current tenancy six months hence).

7.5.1 Landlord's s25 notice

LANDLORD AND TENANT ACT 1954, SECTION 25

**Landlord's Notice to Terminate Business Tenancy***

To (1) O LIMITED

of (2) 22 High Row Marton on Tyne Northumberland

**IMPORTANT – This notice is intended to bring your tenancy to an end. If you want to continue to occupy your property you must act quickly. Read the notice and all the notes carefully. If you are in any doubt about the action you should take, get advice immediately e.g. from a solicitor or surveyor or a citizens advice bureau.**

1 This notice is given under section 25 of the Landlord and Tenant Act 1954.

2 It relates to (3) the premises known as 22 High Row Marton on Tyne

of which you are the tenant.

(4)3 I/We give you notice terminating your tenancy on 5th May 1990

(5)4 Within two months after the giving of this notice, you must notify ~~me~~/us in writing whether or not you are willing to give up possession of the property comprised in the tenancy on the date stated in paragraph 3.

(6)(~~5 If you apply to the court under Part II of the Landlord and Tenant Act1954 for the grant of a new tenancy, I/we will not oppose your application.~~)

(6)(7)[5 If you apply to the court under Part II of the Landlord and Tenant Act 1954 for the grant of a new tenancy, I/we will oppose it on the grounds mentioned in paragraph~~s~~ (f) of section 30(1) of the Act.]

6 All correspondence about this notice should be sent to (8) [~~the landlord~~] [the landlord's agent] at the address given below.

Date 2nd November 1989

Signature of (8) [landlord] [landlord's agent] A Solicitor and Co

Name of landlord A Limited
Address of landlord 1 High Street Worktown

(8)[Address of agent A Solicitor and Co
23 High Street
Worktown
Northumberland]

* This form must *NOT* be used if–
(*a*) no previous notice terminating the tenancy has been given under section 25 of the Act, and
(*b*) the tenancy is the tenancy of a house (as defined for the purposes of Part I of the Leasehold Reform Act 1967), and
(*c*) the tenancy is a long tenancy at a low rent (within the meaning of that Act of 1967), and
(*d*) the tenant is not a company or other artificial person.
If the above apply, use form number 13 [Oyez No. L&T 24] instead of this form.

The following appear as marginal notes on the front of the form.

(1) Name of Tenant.
(2) Address of Tenant.
(3) Description of property.
(4) See notes 1 and 8.
(5) See notes 2 and 3.
(6) The landlord must cross out one version of paragraph 5. If the second version is used the paragraph letter(s) must be filled in.
(7) See notes 4 and 5.
(8) Cross out words in square brackets if they do not apply.

## *NOTES*

*Termination of tenancy*

1 This notice is intended to bring your tenancy to an end. You can apply to the court for a new tenancy under the Landlord and Tenant Act 1954 by following the procedure outlined in notes 2 and 3 below. If you do your tenancy will continue after the date shown in paragraph 3 of this notice while your claim is being considered. The landlord can ask the court to fix the rent which you will have to pay while the tenancy continues. The terms of any *new* tenancy not agreed between you and the landlord will be settled by the court.

*Claiming a new tenancy*

2 If you want to apply to the court for a new tenancy you must:–
(1) notify the landlord in writing not later not later than 2 months after the giving of this notice that you are not willing to give up possession of the property;

**AND**

(2) apply to the court, not earlier than 2 months nor later than 4 months after the giving of this notice, for a new tenancy. You should apply to the County Court unless the rateable value of the business part of your premises is above the current County Court limit. In that case you should apply to the High Court.

(3) The time limits in note 2 run from the giving of the notice. The date of the giving of the notice may not be the date written on the notice or the date on which you actually saw it. It may, for instance, be the date on which the notice was delivered through the post to your last address known to the person giving the notice. If there has been any delay in your seeing this notice you may need to act very quickly. If you are in any doubt get advice immediately.

---

**WARNING TO TENANT**

**If you do not keep to the time limits in Note 2, you will *lose* your right to apply to the court for a new tenancy.**

---

*Landlord's opposition to claim for a new tenancy*

4 If you apply to the court for a new tenancy, the landlord can only oppose your application on one or more of the grounds set out in section 30(1) of the 1954 Act. These grounds are set out below. The paragraph letters are those given in the Act. The landlord can only use a ground if its paragraph letter is shown in paragraph 5 of the notice.

*Grounds*

(*a*) where under the current tenancy the tenant has any obligations as respects the repair and maintenance of the holding, that the tenant ought not to be granted a new tenancy in view of the state of repair of the holding, being a state resulting from the tenant's failure to comply with the said obligations;

(*b*) that the tenant ought not to be granted a new tenancy in view of his persistent delay in paying rent which has become due;

(*c*) that the tenant ought not to be granted a new tenancy in view of other substantial breaches by him of his obligations under the current tenancy, or for any other reason connected with the tenant's use or management of the holding;

(*d*) that the landlord has offered and is willing to provide or secure the provision of alternative accommodation for the tenant, that the terms on which the alternative accommodation is available are reasonable having regard to the terms of the current tenancy and to all other relevant circumstances, and that the accommodation and the time at which it will be available are suitable for the tenant's requirements (including the requirement to preserve goodwill) having regard to the nature and class of his business and to the situation and extent of, and facilities afforded by, the holding;

(*e*) where the current tenancy was created by the sub-letting of part only of the property comprised in a superior tenancy and the landlord is the owner of an interest in reversion expectant on the termination of that superior tenancy, that the aggregate of the rents reasonably obtainable on separate lettings of the holding and the remainder of that property would be substantially less than the rent reasonably obtainable on a letting of that property as a whole, that on the termination of the current tenancy the landlord requires possession of the holding for the purposes of letting or otherwise disposing of the said property as a whole, and that in view thereof the tenant ought not to be granted a new tenancy.

(*f*) that on the termination of the current tenancy the landlord intends to demolish or reconstruct the premises comprised in the holding or a substantial part of those premises or to carry out substantial work of construction on the holding or part thereof and that he could not reasonably do so without obtaining possession of the holding;
(If the landlord used this ground, the court can sometimes still grant a new tenancy if certain conditions set out in section 31A of the Act can be met.)

(*g*) that on the termination of the current tenancy the landlord intends to occupy the holding for the purposes, or partly for the purposes, of a business to be carried on by him therein, or as his residence.
(The landlord must normally have been the landlord for at least five years to use this ground.)

*Compensation*

5 If you cannot get a new tenancy solely because grounds (*e*), (*f*) or (*g*) apply, you are entitled to compensation under the 1954 Act. If your landlord has opposed your application on any of the other grounds as well as (*e*), (*f*) or (*g*) you can only get compensation if the Court's refusal to grant a new tenancy is based solely on grounds (*e*), (*f*) or (*g*). In other words you cannot get compensation under the 1954 Act if the Court has refused your tenancy on *other* grounds even if (*e*), (*f*) or (*g*) also apply.

6 If your landlord is an authority possessing compulsory purchase powers (such as a local authority) you may be entitled to a disturbance payment under Part III of the Land Compensation Act 1973.

*Negotiating a new tenancy*

7 Most leases are renewed by negotiation. If you do try to agree a new tenancy with your landlord, remember–

(1) that your present tenancy will not be extended after the date in paragraph 3 of this notice unless you *both*
(a) give written notice that you will not vacate (note 2(1) above); *and*
(b) apply to the court for a new tenancy (note 2(2) above);

(2) that you will lose your right to apply to the court if you do not keep to the time limits in note 2.

*Validity of the notice*

8 The landlord who has given this notice may not be the landlord to whom you pay your rent. "Business" is given a wide meaning in the 1954 Act and is used in the same sense in this notice. The 1954 Act also has rules about the date which the landlord can put in paragraph 3. This depends on the terms of your tenancy. If you have any doubt about whether this notice is valid, get immediate advice.

*Explanatory booklet*

9 The Department of the Environment and Welsh Office booklet 'Business Tenancies and Security of Tenure' explains the main provisions of Part II of the 1954 Act. It is available from The Department of the Environment Publications Store, Building No 3, Victoria Road, South Ruislip, Middlesex.

### 7.5.2 Tenant's counter-notice

LANDLORD AND TENANT ACT 1954, SECTIONS 25(5) AND 29(2)

**Tenant's Counter-Notice as to Willingness to Give Up Possession of Business Premises**

To (1) A LIMITED

of(2) 1 High Street Worktown Northumberland

we received on (3) 3 November 1989 your notice terminating our tenancy of (4) 22 High Row Marton on Tyne

on (5) 5 May 1990.

TAKE NOTICE that we will [not] (6) be willing to give up possession of the property comprised in the tenancy on that date.

DATED 30 November 1989

Signed: Hopitees

[As solicitor/~~agent~~ for] Tenant

Name of Tenant: O LIMITED

Address of Tenant: 22 High Row Marton on Tyne<br>Northumberland

[Name and address of solicitor/~~agent~~]

Hopitees,
Solicitors,
The Towers,
Worktown,
Northumberland

---

(1) Name of Landlord, see note 1.
(2) Address of Landlord, see note 1.
(3) Date Landlord's notice given, see note 2.
(4) Address of property.
(5) Date given in Landlord's notice.
(6) Delete if Tenant does not wish to apply for a new tenancy, see note 3.

*NOTES*

1 This counter-notice must normally be given to the landlord who served the notice terminating the tenancy, who may not be the immediate landlord to whom the rent is paid. The identity of the landlord to whom the counter-notice has to be given may change: see Landlord and Tenant Act 1954, s 44.

2 This counter-notice must be given within two months of the landlord's notice being given.

3 The tenant cannot apply to the court for a new tenancy unless a counter-notice, stating that he will not be willing to give up possession, has been duly given.

*NB This form is not prescribed and is based upon Oyez Form No L and T 25A.*

### 7.5.3 Tenant's s 26 request

LANDLORD AND TENANT ACT 1954, SECTION 26

**Tenant's Request for New Tenancy of Business Premises**

To (1) A LIMITED

of (2) 1 High Street,
Worktown,
Northumberland

**IMPORTANT – This is a request for a new tenancy of your property or part of it. If you want to oppose this request you must act quickly. Read the request and all the notes carefully. If you are in any doubt about the action you should take, get advice immediately e.g. from a solicitor or surveyor or a citizens advice bureau.**

1 This request is made under section 26 of the Landlord and Tenant Act 1954.

2 You are the landlord of (3) 22 High Row Marton on Tyne Northumberland

3 I/We request you to grant a new tenancy beginning on
1 November 1990

4 I/we propose that:

(a) the property comprised in the new tenancy should be
22 High Row, Marton on Tyne, Northumberland.

(b) the rent payable under the new tenancy should be £10,000 per annum.

(c) the other terms of the new tenancy should be
A term of 5 years with a break clause exercisable by either party serving 3 months notice on the other expiring at the end of the third year of the term but otherwise on the same terms as the current tenancy.

5 All correspondence about this request should be sent to (4) [~~the tenant~~] [the tenant's agent] at the address given below.

Date 2 November 1989

Signature of (4) [~~tenant~~] [tenant's agent] Hopitees

Name of tenant O Limited
Address of tenant 22 High Row Marton on Tyne
Northumberland

(4)[Address of agent] Hopitees,
Solicitors,
The Towers,
Worktown
Northumberland

(1) Name of Landlord.
(2) Address of Landlord.
(3) Description of property.
(4) Cross out words in square brackets if they do not apply.

## *NOTES*

*Request for a new tenancy*

1 This request by your tenant for a new tenancy brings his current tenancy to an end on the day before the date mentioned in paragraph 3 above. He can apply to the court under the Landlord and Tenant Act 1954 for a new tenancy. If he does, his current tenancy will continue after the date mentioned in paragraph 3 of this request while his application is being considered by the court. You can ask the court to fix the rent which your tenant will have to pay whilst his tenancy continues. The terms of any *new* tenancy not agreed between you and your tenant will be settled by the court.

*Opposing a request for a new tenancy*

2 If you do not want to grant a new tenancy, you *must* within two months of the making of this request, give your tenant notice saying that you will oppose any application he makes to the court for a new tenancy. You do not need a special form to do this, but you must state on which of the grounds set out in the 1954 Act you will oppose the application – see note 4.

(3) The time limit in note 2 runs from the making of this request. The date of the making of the request may not be the date written on the request or the date on which you actually saw it. It may, for instance, be the date on which the request was delivered through the post to your last address known to the person giving the request. If there has been any delay in your seeing this request you may need to act very quickly. If you are in any doubt get advice immediately.

**WARNING TO LANDLORD**

**If you do not keep to the time limit in Note 2, you will *lose* your right to oppose your tenant's application to the court for a new tenancy if he makes one.**

*Grounds for opposing an application*

4 If your tenant applies to the court for a new tenancy, you can only oppose the application on one or more of the grounds set out in section 30(1) of the 1954 Act. These grounds are set out below. The paragraph letters are those given in the Act.

*Grounds*

(*a*) where under the current tenancy the tenant has any obligations as respects the repair and maintenance of the holding, that the tenant ought not to be granted a new tenancy in view of the state of repair of the holding, being a state resulting from the tenant's failure to comply with the said obligations;

(*b*) that the tenant ought not to be granted a new tenancy in view of his persistent delay in paying rent which has become due;

(*c*) that the tenant ought not to be granted a new tenancy in view of other substantial breaches by him of his obligations under the current tenancy, or for any other reason connected with the tenant's use or management of the holding;

(*d*) that you have offered and are willing to provide or secure the provision of alternative accommodation for the tenant, that the terms on which the alternative accommodation is available are reasonable having regard to the terms of the current tenancy and to all other relevant circumstances, and that the accommodation and the time at which it will be available are suitable for the tenant's requirements (including the requirement to preserve goodwill) having regard to the nature and class of his business and to the situation and extent of, and facilities afforded by, the holding;

(*e*) where the current tenancy was created by the sub-letting of part only of the property comprised in a superior tenancy and you are the owner of an interest in reversion expectant on the termination of that superior tenancy, that the aggregate of the rents reasonably obtainable on separate lettings of the holding and the remainder of that property would be substantially less than the rent reasonably obtainable on a letting of that property as a whole, that on the termination of the current tenancy you require possession of the holding for the purpose of letting or otherwise disposing of the said property as a whole, and that in view thereof the tenant ought not to be granted a new tenancy;

(*f*) that on the termination of the current tenancy you intend to demolish or reconstruct the premises comprised in the holding or a substantial part of those premises or to carry out substantial work of construction on the holding or part thereof and that you could not reasonably do so without obtaining possession of the holding;

(If you use this ground, the court can sometimes still grant a new tenancy if certain conditions set out in section 31A of the Act can be met.)

(*g*) that on the termination of the current tenancy you intend to occupy the holding for the purposes, or partly for the purposes, of a business to be carried on by him therein, or as your residence.

(You must normally have been the landlord for at least five years to use this ground.)

You can only use one or more of the above grounds if you have stated them in the notice referred to in note 2 above.

*Compensation*

5 If your tenant cannot get a new tenancy solely because ground (*e*), (*f*), or (*g*), apply, he is entitled to compensation from you under the 1954 Act. If you have opposed his application on any of the other grounds as well as (*e*), (*f*), or (*g*), he can only get compensation if the court's refusal to grant a new tenancy is based solely on grounds (*e*), (*f*), or (*g*). In other words he cannot get compensation under the 1954 Act if the court has refused his tenancy on *other* grounds even if (*e*), (*f*), or (*g*) also apply.

6 If you are an authority possessing compulsory purchase power (such as a local authority) you will be aware that your tenant may be entitled to a disturbance payment under Part III of the Land Compensation Act 1973.

*Negotiating a new tenancy*

7 Most leases are renewed by negotiation. If you do try to agree a new tenancy with your tenant–

(1) YOU should remember that you will not be able to oppose an application to the court for a new tenancy unless you give the notice mentioned in note 2 above within the time limit in that note;

(2) YOUR TENANT should remember that he will lose his right to apply to the court for a new tenancy unless he makes the application not less than two nor more than four months after the making of this request.

*Validity of this notice*

8 The landlord to whom this request is made may not be the landlord to whom the tenant pays the rent. "Business" is given a wide meaning in the 1954 Act and is used in the same sense in this request. The 1954 Act also has rules about the date which the tenant can put in paragraph 3. This

depends on the terms of the tenancy. If you have any doubts about whether this request is valid, get immediate advice.

*Explanatory booklet*

9 The Department of the Environment and Welsh Office booklet 'Business Tenancies and Security of Tenure' explains the main provisions of Part II of the 1954 Act. It is available from The Department of the Environment Publications Store, Building No 3, Victoria Road, South Ruislip, Middlesex.

### 7.5.4 Landlord's counter-notice

LANDLORD AND TENANT ACT 1954, SECTION 26(6)

**Landlord's Notice Opposing Grant of New Tenancy of Business Premises**

To (1) O LIMITED

of(2) 22 High Row Marton on Tyne Northumberland

I/we received on (3) 3 November 1989 your request for a new tenancy of (4) 22 High Row, Marton on Tyne, Northumberland

TAKE NOTICE that I/we shall oppose an application to the court for the grant of a new tenancy on the grounds mentioned in paragraph (5) (f) of section 30(1) of the Landlord and Tenant Act 1954, as set out overleaf in Note 3 to this notice.

DATED 30 November 1989

Signed: A Solicitor and Co

As solicitor for the Landlord

Name of Landlord: A Limited

Address of Landlord: 1 High Street,
Worktown

[Name and address of solicitor]

A Solicitor and Co.
23 High Street,
Worktown

(1) Name of Tenant.
(2) Address of Tenant.
(3) Date Tenant's request made, see note 1.
(4) Address of property.
(5) Insert paragraph letter(s), see note 2.

## *NOTES*

1 A landlord who wishes to oppose an application to the court by the tenant for a new tenancy must serve this notice within two months of the tenant making his request.

2 The grounds upon which the landlord may oppose an application to the court are limited to those set out in Note 3. The landlord can only rely on grounds specified in this notice, by the insertion of the appropriate paragraph letter(s). References to more than one ground may be inserted.

3 The grounds on which the landlord may oppose the tenant's application, as specified in the Landlord and Tenant Act 1954, s30(1), are:

*Grounds*

(*a*) where under the current tenancy the tenant has any obligations as respects the repair and maintenance of the holding, that the tenant ought not to be granted a new tenancy in view of the state of repair of the holding, being a state resulting from the tenant's failure to comply with the said obligations;

(*b*) that the tenant ought not to be granted a new tenancy in view of his persistent delay in paying rent which has become due;

(*c*) that the tenant ought not to be granted a new tenancy in view of other substantial breaches by him of his obligations under the current tenancy, or for any other reason connected with the tenant's use or management of the holding;

(*d*) that the landlord has offered and is willing to provide or secure the provision of alternative accommodation for the tenant, that the terms on which the alternative accommodation is available are reasonable having regard to the terms of the current tenancy and to all other relevant circumstances, and that the accommodation and the time at which it will be available are suitable for the tenant's requirements (including the requirement to preserve goodwill) having regard to the nature and class of his business and to the situation and extent of, and facilities afforded by, the holding;

(*e*) where the current tenancy was created by the sub-letting of part only of the property comprised in a superior tenancy and the landlord is the owner of an interest in reversion expectant on the termination of that superior tenancy, that the aggregate of the rents reasonably obtainable on separate lettings of the holding and the remainder of that property would be substantially less than the rent reasonably obtainable on a letting of that property as a whole, that on the termination of the current tenancy the landlord requires possession of the holding for the purposes of letting or otherwise disposing of the said property as a whole, and that in view thereof the tenant ought not to be granted a new tenancy;

(*f*) that on the termination of the current tenancy the landlord intends to demolish or reconstruct the premises comprised in the holding or a substantial part of those premises or to carry out substantial work of construction on the holding or part thereof and that he could not reasonably do so without obtaining possession of the holding;

(*g*) that on the termination of the current tenancy the landlord intends to occupy the holding for the purposes, or partly for the purposes, of a business to be carried on by him therein, or as his residence.

4 In section 30(1), quoted in Note 3, 'the holding' means the property comprised in the tenancy, other than any which is occupied neither by the tenant nor by someone whom he employs for the purposes of a business which brings the tenancy within the scope of the Landlord and Tenant Act 1954: s23(3).

*NB This form is not prescribed and is based upon Oyez Form No L and T 27.*

### 7.5.5 Request for originating application in the county court

THE MARTON ON TYNE COUNTY COURT

**No of Matter XY 123**

BETWEEN

O LIMITED Applicant

and

A LIMITED Respondent

We hereby request that the accompanying originating application be issued in accordance with the instructions therein:–

Dated this Tenth day of February 1990.

(*Signed*)

*Applicant's solicitor* Hopitees

Address The Towers,
Worktown,
Northumberland

To the Registrar.

### 7.5.6 Tenant's originating application

THE MARTON ON TYNE COUNTY COURT

No of Matter XY 123

**In the matter of the Landlord and Tenant Act 1954**

**and**

**In the matter of** the lease of the premises known as 22 High Row Marton on Tyne Northumberland

BETWEEN

O LIMITED Applicant

and

A LIMITED Respondent

1 We O LIMITED

of 22 High Row Marton on Tyne Northumberland
apply to the court for the grant of a new tenancy pursuant to Part II of the Landlord and Tenant Act 1954.

2 The premises to which this application relates are:–
(1) 22 High Row Marton on Tyne Northumberland

3 The rateable value of the premises is:–
£2,300

4 The nature of the business carried on at the premises is:–
A newsagents and confectioner's shop

5 The following are the particulars of our current tenancy of the premises:–
(*a*) (*Date of lease or agreement for a lease or tenancy agreement*) 1 April 1985
(*b*) (*Names of parties to lease or agreement*)
A LIMITED (1) and
O LIMITED (2).
(*c*) (*Term granted by lease or agreement*) 5 years from and including 1 April 1985
(*d*) (*Rent reserved by lease or agreement*) £6,000 per annum
(*e*) (*Terms as to date and mode of termination of tenancy*)

Break clause exercisable by landlord serving three months notice expiring on 31 March 1988 and usual rights of re-entry upon tenant's breach of covenant.

(*f*) *(Whether any and, if so, what part of the property comprised in the tenancy is occupied neither by the tenant, nor by a person employed by the tenant for the purposes of the business carried on by the tenant in the premises)*

None

---

(1) Give address of premises.

(ALTERNATIVE WHERE LANDLORD SERVED A S 25 NOTICE (7.5.1))

6 On 3 November 1989 the Respondent served on us a notice to terminate dated in accordance with the provisions of section 25 of the Act giving 5 May 1990 as the date for termination and stating that the Respondent would [~~not~~] oppose application to this Court for a new tenancy.

On 2 December 1989 We served on the Respondent:–
a counter-notice dated 30th November 1989 stating that We would not be willing to give up possession of the premises on the date of termination.

7 The following are our proposals as to the period, rent and other terms of the new tenancy for which we are applying:–

A term of 5 years at a rent of £10,000 per annum with a break clause exercisable by either party serving 3 months notice on the other expiring at the end of the third year of the term but otherwise on the same terms as the current tenancy.

8 (3) The following persons are to our knowledge interested in reversion in the premises on the termination of our current tenancy:–

None

9 (4) The following other persons have to our knowledge an interest in the premises other than a freehold interest and are likely to be affected by the grant of a new tenancy:–

None

10 The names and address of the Respondent on whom this application is intended to be served are:–

A Limited of
1 High Street,
Worktown,
Northumberland.

11 Our address for service is:–

Hopitees,
The Towers,
Worktown,
Northumberland.

Dated this 10 day of February, 1990.

*Solicitor for the Applicant*

Hopitees, The Towers,
Worktown, Northumberland.

---

(1) Give address of premises.
(2) Delete whichever sentence in square brackets is inapplicable.
(3) Give names and addresses and nature of interest in the premises (whether immediately or in not more than 14 years), of persons other than the Respondent.
(4) Give names and addresses and nature of interest.

(ALTERNATIVE WHERE LANDLORD SERVED A S 26 REQUEST (7.5.3)

6 On 3 November 1989 We served on the Respondent:–
a request dated 2 November 1989 for a new tenancy in accordance with the provisions of section 26 of the Act specifying 1 November 1990 as the date for commencement of the new tenancy. ~~(2) [The Respondent has not served on us any counter notice.~~] [On 2nd December 1989 the Respondent served on us a counter-notice dated 30th November 1989 stating that it would oppose an application to the court for the grant of a new tenancy.]

7 The following are our proposals as to the period, rent and other terms of the new tenancy for which we are applying:–

A term of 5 years at a rent of £10,000 per annum with a break clause exercisable by either party serving 3 months notice on the other expiring at the end of the third year of the term but otherwise on the same terms as the current tenancy.

8 (3) The following persons are to our knowledge interested in reversion in the premises on the termination of our current tenancy:–

None

9 (4) The following other persons have to our knowledge an interest in the premises other than a freehold interest and are likely to be affected by the grant of a new tenancy:–

None

10 The names and address of the Respondent on whom this application is intended to be served are:–

A Limited of
1 High Street,
Worktown,
Northumberland.

11 Our address for service is:–

Hopitees,
The Towers,
Worktown,
Northumberland.

Dated this 10 day of February, 1990.

*Solicitor for the Applicant*
Hopitees, The Towers,
Worktown, Northumberland.

---

(2) Delete whichever sentence in square brackets is inapplicable.
(3) Give names and addresses and nature of interest in the premises (whether immediately or in not more than 14 years), of persons other than the Respondent.
(4) Give names and addresses and nature of interest.

*Note*

The action must be commenced by originating application (CCR Ord 43, r 2 (1)). The applicant files in the appropriate court:

(a) A self-addressed envelope where issuing through the post

(b) A request

(c) An originating application and copy for each other party

(d) A cheque for £30.00

(e) A request for service to be made by the applicant (if required)

If the applicant does not request service, the court will automatically serve a notice and copy of the application upon the respondent by first class post (CCR Ord 7, r 10(1) and Ord 3, r 4(6)). A plaint note is sent to the applicant.

Where the papers are served by the court, the date of service shall, unless the contrary is shown, be deemed to be the seventh day after the date on which the application was sent to the respondent (CCR Ord 7, r 10(3)). The application must be served within two months of its issue or within such further period as the court may allow (CCR Ord 7, r 20(1) and (2) and Ord 43, r6(3)). It is very important that the originating application be served in time. If following judgment or the making of an order, it appears to the court that the process did not come to the notice of the respondent in time the judgment or order can be set aside (CCR Ord 37, r 3). Personal service may therefore be preferred rather than relying on postal service by an officer of the court.

On issuing the orginating application the court will usually adjourn the matter generally with liberty to either party to apply to fix a hearing date. If no application is made within twelve months the court may give notice that, unless either party applies within fourteen days for a date or adjournment, the matter will be struck out (CCR Ord 13, r 3).

### 7.5.7 Landlord's answer

THE MARTON ON TYNE COUNTY COURT

**No of Matter** XY 123

**In the matter of the Landlord and Tenant Act 1954**

**In the matter of** the lease of the premises known as 22 High Row, Marton on Tyne, Northumberland

BETWEEN

O LIMITED Applicant

and

A LIMITED Respondent

WE, A LIMITED

of 1 High Street, Worktown, Northumberland
the respondent in this matter, in answer to the application of

O LIMITED for a new tenancy of the premises known as
22 High Row, Marton on Tyne, Northumberland say that:–

(1) 1 [~~We do not oppose the grant of a new tenancy~~]

We oppose the grant of a new tenancy on the following grounds stated in our notice under sections [25] [26(6)] of the Act, namely:–
(2)

The ground mentioned in paragraph (f) of section 30(1) of the Act.

(1) 2 [~~If a new tenancy is granted we do not object to its being granted on the terms proposed by the Applicant~~]

If a new tenancy is granted, we object to its being granted on the following terms proposed by the Applicant, namely:–
(3)

A rent of £10,000 per annum and a break clause exercisable by either party serving 3 months notice on the other expiring at the end of the third year of the term.

and the following are our counter-proposals as to the period, rent and other terms of such a tenancy:–

A rent of £15,000 per annum and a break clause exercisable by the landlord only serving 3 months notice expiring at the end of the third year of the term but otherwise on the same terms as the current tenancy.

(1) 3 We are not a tenant under a lease having less than 14 years unexpired at the date of termination of the Applicant's current tenancy.

[~~We are a tenant under a lease having less than 14 years unexpired at the date of termination of the Applicant's current tenancy and the name and address of the person(s) having an interest in the reversion~~

~~expectant on the termination of the Respondent's tenancy immediately or within not more than 14 years of the date of such termination [is] [are]~~] (4)

4 The following persons are to our knowledge likely to be affected by the grant of a new tenancy:–
(5)

None

(6) 5 [~~We require that any new tenancy ordered to be granted shall be a tenancy of the whole of the property comprised in the Applicant's current tenancy~~]

6 We hereby apply to the court under section 24A of the Act to determine a rent which would be reasonable for the Applicant to pay while the tenancy continues by virtue of section 24 of the Act.

Dated this 17 day of February 1990

*Solicitor for the Respondent*
A Solicitor and Co.
23 High Street,
Worktown,
Northumberland.

(1) Strike out statement which does not apply.
(2) Here set out the grounds.
(3) Here state the terms to which you object.
(4) Here set out the names and addresses of any reversioners.
(5) Here set out the names, addresses and nature of the interests in the premises of all persons, other than a freeholder or a tenant, who are likely to be so affected.
(6) If the applicant's current tenancy is one to which section 32(2) of the Act applies, add, if you so require.

*Note*

An answer must be filed (CCR Ord 43, r 2 (1)). This must be done within fourteen days after service of the application accompanied by as many copies as there are other parties to the proceedings (CCR Ord 9, r 18(3)). The court will send a copy to the applicant and to every other party (CCR Ord 9, r 18(4)).

The fourteen day period may be extended by consent of both parties who may wish to do this where negotiations for a new lease are advanced (CCR Ord 13, r 4).

### 7.5.8 Notice of discontinuance

IN THE MARTON ON TYNE COUNTY COURT

NO OF MATTER XY 123

IN THE MATTER OF THE LANDLORD AND TENANT ACT 1954

and

IN THE MATTER OF THE LEASE OF THE PREMISES KNOWN AS 22 HIGH ROW MARTON ON TYNE NORTHUMBERLAND

Between

O LIMITED Applicant

and

A LIMITED Respondent

TAKE NOTICE that the Applicant hereby wholly discontinues this action as against the Respondent (and we certify that we have today given the like notice to the Respondent).

Dated this Eighth day of March 1990

SIGNED ..........................................................................................
Solicitors for the Applicant

To the Registrar

*Note*

The tenant will usually withdraw the application if agreement is reached (see *3.1.4)*.The tenant must give notice to the landlord and to the court (CCR Ord 18, r 1). The court's copy must contain a certificate that the applicant has also given notice to the respondent.

Any compromise reached between the parties should deal with the question of costs.

# 7.6 Declaration that the Landlord has unreasonably withheld consent to assignment of lease and change of user

## 7.6.1 Originating application

IN THE WORKTOWN COUNTY COURT MATTER NO.

In the Matter of Section 53 of
the Landlord and Tenant Act 1954

and

In the Matter of a Lease Dated
20th August 1989 of Premises
Known as 45 High Street Worktown

Between

X LIMITED Applicant

and

WALTER SMITH Respondent

**Originating Application**

1. X Limited, applies to the Court for an order in the following terms:
   (i) A declaration that the Respondent has unreasonably withheld his consent under the Lease dated 20th August 1989 ('the Lease') of the premises known as 45 High Street Worktown ('the Premises') to the assignment of the residue unexpired of the term created by the Lease by the Applicant to Jane Jones ('the Assignee') and that the Applicant is entitled to assign the Lease to the Assignee notwithstanding the refusal of the Respondent to give his consent to such assignment.
   (ii) A declaration that the Respondent has unreasonably withheld his consent under the Lease to the proposed user of the Premises for the provision of financial services and that upon the assignment of the Lease to the Assignee, the Assignee would be entitled to use the Premises for that purpose notwithstanding the absence of the Respondent's consent.
2. The grounds on which the Applicant claims to be entitled to the order are as follows:

(i) The Premises were demised by the Respondent to the Applicant by the Lease for a term of 10 years from 20th August 1989 and the reversion immediately expectant upon the term is still vested in the Respondent.

(ii) By clause 2(15) of the Lease the Applicant covenanted as follows:

'Not to . . . assign . . . the whole of the Premises . . . without the consent in writing of the Landlord (the Respondent) first obtained which consent shall not be unreasonably withheld . . .'

(iii) By clause 2(18) of the Lease the Applicant further covenanted as follows:

'Not to use or permit to be used the Premises for any purpose other than as a travel agency or such other use as may first be approved in writing by the Landlord (the Respondent) which approval shall not be unreasonably withheld . . .'

(iv) By a letter to the Respondent dated 3rd October 1989 the Applicant asked for the consent of the Respondent to the proposed assignment of the Lease to the Assignee and to the proposed change of use and on 19th October 1989 forwarded to the Respondent two trade references and one bank reference relating to the Assignee all of which stated that the Assignee would be an excellent tenant. By a letter to the Applicant dated 8th November 1989 the Respondent refused his consent to the proposed assignment and change of use on the basis that the proposed use of the Assignee for the provision of financial services would adversely affect the rental value of the Premises and adjoining property owned by the Respondent.

(v) The Respondent's refusal of consent to the proposed assignment to the Assignee and to the proposed change of use is unreasonable and the Applicant is entitled to the declarations asked for in this application for the following reasons:

(a) The Assignee is a respectable and responsible person who has operated successfully in the field of the provision of financial services from other premises

(b) The provision of financial services is a similar type of service user to the existing user of the Premises as a travel agency and will therefore have the same affect on the rental value of the Premises and adjoining property owned by the Respondent as the said existing user

3. The names and address of the person on whom it is intended to serve this application is Walter Smith whose address is 44 The Avenue Newtown
4. The Applicant's address for service is c/o Messrs Hopitees, The Towers, Worktown

DATED this Fourth day of December 1989

..........................................................................................

Solicitors for the Applicant

*Note*

The action is commenced by originating application (CCR Ord 43 r 2(1)) (see notes to Precedent *7.5.6* for documents to be filed and method of service). The application must be served within 12 months of its issue (CCR Ord 7 r 20(1)).

### 7.6.2 Answer to originating application

IN THE WORKTOWN COUNTY COURT MATTER NO. XY334

In the Matter of section 53 of
the Landlord and Tenant Act 1954

and

In the Matter of a Lease Dated the
20th August 1989 of Premises Known
as 45 High Street Worktown

Between

X LIMITED Applicant

and

WALTER SMITH Respondent

**Answer**

I WALTER SMITH of 44 The Avenue Newtown in answer to the Originating Application of X Limited whose registered office is at the Grange Worktown, say that:

1. My refusal to permit the assignment of the lease to Jane Jones and to permit the Premises to be used for the provision of financial services was made for the following reasons:
    (i) Jane Jones is a former bankrupt and the references supplied do not contain sufficient information to indicate clearly that she would not again fall into financial difficulties
    (ii) The business of providing financial services would detract from the other high quality users in the Respondent's adjoining properties and would lead to a diminution in the market rents both of the Premises and the Respondent's adjoining properties and/or a diminution in value of the Respondent's reversionary interests in the Premises and adjoining properties
    (iii) An assignment to Jane Jones is likely to cause discontent amongst retail tenants of the Respondent's adjoining properties who have their own schemes for providing credit to their customers and may cause some of these tenants to leave these properties
2. I dispute paragraph 2(v) of the Originating Application for the reasons pleaded in paragraph 1 herein
3. In the circumstances it was reasonable to withhold consent

DATED this Thirteenth day of December 1989

.....................................................................................................
Solicitors for the Respondent

To: the Registrar and
to the Applicant

The Respondent's address for service is c/o Messrs A Solicitor and Co 23 High Street Worktown

*Note*
The respondent must file an answer within 14 days after service of the application (CCR Ord 43 r 2(1) and see notes to Precedent 7.5.7)

## 7.7 Licence permitting assignment

THIS LICENCE is made the First day of October 1989 BETWEEN the party whose name and address is set out in Part I of the FIRST

SCHEDULE hereto ('the Landlord') of the first part the party whose names and addresses are set out in Part II of that Schedule ('the Tenant') of the second part and the party whose name and address is set out in Part III of that Schedule ('the Assignee') of the third part and is SUPPLEMENTAL to the Lease ('the Lease') referred to in the SECOND SCHEDULE hereto whereby the premises ('the Premises') briefly described in that Schedule were demised for the term of years ('the Term') referred to in that Schedule subject to the payment of the rents reserved by and the performance and observance of the covenants on the lessee's part and the conditions contained in the Lease.

NOW THIS DEED WITNESSETH as follows:

1. The Landlord grants to the Tenant licence to assign all the estate and interest of the Tenant in the Premises to the Assignee
2. The Assignee covenants with the Landlord that throughout the residue of the Term the Assignee will pay the rents and other sums of money reserved and made payable by the Lease including increased rent arising on review pursuant to the provisions in that behalf contained in the Lease and observe and perform the covenants on the part of the lessee and the conditions therein contained
3. The Tenant covenants with the Landlord that the Tenant will pay the Landlord's reasonable and proper costs of and in connection with this Deed including those arising from the consideration of the application for and preparation and completion of this Deed
4. If the assignment hereby authorised shall not have been implemented and the Deed of Assignment or a certified copy thereof produced to the Landlord's Solicitors within two months from the date hereof then the licence granted by Clause 1 hereof shall be absolutely void and of no effect but without liability on the part of the Landlord arising out of or incidental to this Deed
5. The proviso for re-entry contained in the Lease shall be exercisable by the Landlord as well on breach by the Assignee of any of the provisions herein contained as on the happening of any of the events mentioned in such proviso
6. In this Licence where the context admits the expression 'the Landlord' shall include the persons from time to time entitled in reversion immediately expectant on the Term and the expression 'the Assignee' shall include the persons deriving title under the Assignee and where the expressions 'the Tenant' and 'the Assignee' comprise two or more persons the obligations of the Tenant and the Assignee respectively shall be construed as joint and several

IN WITNESS whereof the parties hereto have hereunto set their hands and seals the day and year first before written

THE FIRST SCHEDULE

PART I

HORACE SCOTT of Viewforth Ashtown North Yorkshire
The Landlord

PART II

ALICE WHITE of 4 Town View Ashtown North Yorkshire
The Tenant

PART III

JENNIFER FROCK of 36 Milburn Street Ashtown North Yorkshire
The Assignee

THE SECOND SCHEDULE

PARTICULARS OF THE LEASE

| | | |
|---|---|---|
| Date | : | 29th September 1969 |
| The parties | : | Horace Scott (1) Neville Shepherd (2) |
| The premises | : | 113 High Row Ashtown North Yorkshire |
| The term | : | 25 years |

SIGNED SEALED AND DELIVERED
by the said HORACE SCOTT
in the presence of:

SIGNED SEALED AND DELIVERED
by the said ALICE WHITE
in the presence of:

SIGNED SEALED AND DELIVERED
by the said JENNIFER FROCK
in the presence of:

*Note*
In the absence of clause 2 the Assignee would only be liable for breaches of the covenants in the lease (touching and concerning the premises) occurring during her period of ownership. A prospective assignee may argue that such an extension of liablity is not a reasonable requirement under s 19(1) of the 1927 Act (see *6.2.2*).

## 7.8 Deed of surrender of a registered lease

HM LAND REGISTRY
Land Registration Acts 1925 to 1971

| | |
|---|---|
| County and District | Durham – Dunelm |
| Title Number | ABC 54321 |
| Property | 2 Commercial Row Dunelm |
| Landlord | Joseph Wood of 24 High Road Dunelm |
| Tenant | Nancy Knight of 44 The Avenue Dunelm |
| Date | |

For the purpose of surrendering the term comprised in the registered title and in consideration of the sum of Fifteen thousand pounds (£15,000) together with Value Added Tax payable thereon (the receipt of which sums is hereby acknowledged) the Tenant as beneficial owner hereby transfers and surrenders to the Landlord the land comprised in Title No ABC 54321 to the intent that the residue of the term of years granted by the registered lease and any other estate interest or right of the Tenant in such land whether granted by or arising from such lease or deed or document supplemental thereto ('the Leasehold Documents') may merge and be extinguished in the reversion thereof (comprised in title No ABC 12345).

The Landlord and the Tenant (a) each release the other from all obligations and liabilities whether past present and future arising from the Leasehold Documents, and (b) both apply to the Chief Land Registrar to make the relevant entries and cancellations on Title Numbers ABC 54321 and ABC 12345 and agree to lodge their Land Certificates at HM Land Registry for this purpose.

It is hereby certified that the transaction hereby effected does not form part of a larger transaction or series of transactions in respect of which the amount or value or aggregate amount or value of the consideration exceeds £30,000.

SIGNED SEALED AND DELIVERED
by the said JOSEPH WOOD
in the presence of:

SIGNED SEALED AND DELIVERED
by the said NANCY KNIGHT
in the presence of:

*Note*
An express surrender of a registered lease takes the form of a transfer. Simple amendments to this precedent will be required if there is no monetary consideration or the reversion is not registered.

The surrender for a consideration of an interest in land is standard rated for Value Added Tax and the deed must therefore state that VAT is payable on the consideration (see *1.7*).

CHAPTER 8

# COMMON PRACTICAL PROBLEMS

1. *A company needs to take occupation immediately of office premises to be held on a five-year lease. I act for the prospective landlord who tells me that he may wish to redevelop the site within the next three to five years. How can I ensure that he will be able to recover possession when he requires it for redevelopment?*

   Advice A break clause should be inserted into the draft lease allowing the landlord to terminate the five-year term early at any time after three years of the term have elapsed, by serving say six months' notice to quit on the tenant, this option being stated to be exercisable only in a situation where the landlord wishes to redevelop. If the 1954 Act applies, then the notice will have to be in the form specified by s 25 of that Act. The tenant has the right to serve a counter-notice and apply to the court for a new tenancy. The landlord will only be able to obtain possession if he can prove ground (f) (see *3.1.5*). The landlord should, therefore, obtain the tenant's agreement and, before the lease commences, apply to the court under s 38(4) of the 1954 Act for an order that the Act should not apply (see *7.4*). This will ensure that the landlord will obtain possession quickly (if required) rather than having to follow the procedures of the 1954 Act.

2. *I act for a tenant of business premises holding on a quarterly periodic tenancy who has just received a letter from her landlord requiring her to vacate the premises on the quarter day falling three months after my client received this letter. Must she leave on this date?*

   Advice Whereas the notice to quit would suffice at common law to determine the tenancy, the effect of the 1954 Act (if applicable) is that the landlord must serve a notice under s 25 of that Act specifying a termination date at least six months hence. The tenant cannot therefore be required to leave on the date specified in the ordinary notice to quit. The tenant unfortunately cannot serve her own request for a new tenancy under s 26 commencing twelve months hence as she does not have a fixed term exceeding one year (*3.1.3*).

3. *My client has a nine-year lease which would (if there was not a statutory continuation under the 1954 Act) expire in six months' time. The landlord, who bought the reversion three years ago, has indicated that he wishes to occupy the premises himself at the earliest possible moment, but has not yet served a notice on the tenant. My client wishes to remain in the premises. How can I best protect his position?*

   Advice The tenant should serve a s 26 request for a new tenancy commencing twelve months after service. Provided that this commencement date is before the date when the landlord has been a landlord by purchase for five years the landlord will not be able to rely upon ground (g) (see *3.1.5*).

4. *My client is building a small shopping centre. How can he restrict the user of each unit so as to achieve a good mix of service and retail occupiers while maximising the rental return from the centre?*

   Advice The landlord should restrict each tenant's user in the lease as appropriate but provide that, for the purposes of rent review, the permitted user is assumed to be any retail user (apart from those retail users likely to depress rentals). There will need to be additional assumptions that the hypothetical user is lawful and that the premises have been adapted for this user. Too wide a variation between the actual and hypothetical permitted users can lead to difficult valuation problems if not dealt with at the drafting stage.

5. *One of the prospective tenants of the shopping centre referred to above is a company and a desirable tenant in all respects save for the fact that, as it has only been trading for two years, there is no evidence that it is of sufficient substance to meet its obligations. Are there any drafting techniques which can be used which may minimise the risk of the landlord suffering financial loss because of the tenant's default?*

   Advice If the directors (or other persons willing to accept the risk) are of sufficient substance then they can be joined into the lease to give personal guarantees. The lease should provide that the guarantors will, in the event of disclaimer by the liquidator of the company, accept a lease on the same terms, that the proviso for re-entry will also apply where a guarantor has become bankrupt and that the guarantee extends to a period of continuation at the end of the tenancy under the 1954 Act. The personal guarantees will extend even after the original tenant has assigned its interest and it may facilitate obtaining sureties if the lease provides for their release if the assignee is of sufficient substance or equivalent guarantees are given.

   An alternative is for the tenant to deposit a sum of money in a bank account to be released to the landlord to compensate him for breaches of covenant. Again, there may be provision in the rent deposit agreement for the sum to be released if an assignee is of sufficient substance or equivalent guarantees are given.

CHAPTER 9

# FURTHER READING

## 9.1 Looseleaf works

Such works have become popular in recent years and now include:

Aldridge, *Leasehold Law* (Longman)
Aldridge, *Practical Lease Precedents* (Longman)
Bernstein and Reynolds, *Handbook of Rent Review* (Sweet & Maxwell)
*Emmet on Title,* 19th edn (Longman)
Hill and Redman, *Landlord and Tenant,* 18th edn (Butterworths)
Reynolds and Clark, *Renewal of Business Tenancies Law and Practice* (HS Publications)
Williams Brand and Hubbard, *Handbook of Business Tenancies* (Sweet & Maxwell)
*Woodfall's Law of Landlord and Tenant,* 28th edn (Sweet & Maxwell)

All of the above works are excellent and a selection, taking into account the fact that some cover similar ground, should be on all practitioners' shelves.

## 9.2 Books

The following books may prove useful especially those marked with an asterisk:

⋆Aldridge *Letting Business Premises,* 5th edn (Longman, 1985)
⋆Atkin's Court Forms, Vol 24, 2nd edn (Butterworths, 1981) and current Annual Supplement.
Beaumont, *Rent Review,* 1st edn (Blackwell Scientific, 1987)
Brahams, *Commercial Leases,* 1st edn (Blackwell Scientific, 1985)
Brand, *Planning Law,* 1st edn (Longman, 1989)
⋆Brand and Williams, *Planning Law for Conveyancers,* 2nd edn (Longman, 1987)
⋆Butterworths, *Landlord and Tenant Handbook,* 2nd edn (Butterworths, 1987)
⋆Clark and Adams, *Rent Reviews and Variable Rents,* 3rd edn (Longman, 1989)

*Coates, *Conveyancing,* 1st edn (Longman, 1988)

*Encyclopaedia of Forms and Precedents, Vol 22, 5th edn (Butterworths 1986)

Freedman and Shapiro, *Service Charges Law and Practice,* 1st edn (HS Publications, 1986)

*Lewison, *Drafting Business Leases,* 3rd edn (Longman, 1989)

***Longman Directory of Local Authorities 1988/89**

O'Hare, *Moeran's Practical Conveyancing,* 11th edn (Longman, 1989)

*Ross, *Drafting and Negotiating Commercial Leases,* 2nd edn (Butterworths, 1984)

Silverman, *Conveyancing Searches and Enquiries,* 1st edn (Butterworths, 1985)

Timothy, *Wotner's Guide to Land Registry Practice,* 16th edn (Longman, 1987)

Walter and Harris, *Claims to the Possession of Land: The Law and Practice,* 1st edn (Fourmat Publishing, 1987)

Wilkinson, *Standard Conditions of Sale of Land,* 3rd edn (Longman, 1982)

Yates and Hawkins, *Landlord and Tenant Law,* 2nd edn (Sweet & Maxwell, 1986)

## 9.3 Journals

The *Estates Gazette* is essential reading for anyone specialising in this field of law being a specialist landlord and tenant journal. The Law Society's *Gazette* will also be useful.